Wake
of the
Whale

≈

Alice Kinsella & Daniel Wade

Mayo
Books
Press

Wake *of the* Whale

Alice Kinsella & Daniel Wade

Published in Ireland in 2024 by

Mayo Books Press

Castlebar, County Mayo

Design and layout:
SiobhanFoody.com

ISBN 978-1-914596-26-1

With thanks to:

Praise for *Wake of the Whale*

"An utterly brilliant and visual-physical-poetical exploration of the fate and mortal beauty of the whale in Irish waters. All the pity and majesty of their existence, and ours, is laid bare in Alice Kinsella's dreamlike work which, like Melville's *Moby-Dick* before it, defies all description and arouses the deepest empathy."

– **Philip Hoare**, author of *Leviathan or, the Whale*

"A lucid and enthralling exploration of whales and whaling, while also a poetic, personal journey. *Wake of the Whale* is like no other book. Unpredictable and exciting as the sea, the pages permeate every aspect of our culture, personal and political. Reading it is like being in an enchanted dream. This is an important, enthralling and genre bending book."

- **Anja Murray**, author of *The Wild Embrace*

"If we are to honour nature we need to confront the sins of the past. This bold and timely truth-telling regarding Ireland's less-than-honourable treatment of whales over the centuries feels like a first step towards healing."

– **Manchán Magan**, author of *Listen to the Land Speak*

"In this deeply moving and richly researched book, Alice Kinsella and Daniel Wade, uncover the haunting and harrowing tale of our troubled relationships with *an míol mór* — our ancient sea kin, the whale. Weaving together poignant threads of personal experience, fascinating archival material, poetry and diverse knowledges, this book moves us to reconsider the deeply interdependent relationship between humans and whales."

– **Dr Easkey Britton**, author of *Saltwater in the Blood* and *Ebb and Flow*

"Kinsella and Wade's magnificent new book extends the tradition of sea-shanty singers, Melville's classic novel, and a deep history of whaling as cultural practice into the 21st century. Newsclips, archival photographs, poetry, and political challenges to preserving the Anthropocene all fuse together to tell us an essential new tale from 'the sea [that] has a thousand spouts'."

– **Mark Nowak**, author of *Coal Mountain Elementary*

In memory of

Dr Roger Payne
1935-2023

Dr James Fairley
1940-2023

The 894 whales who lost their lives in Mayo waters
in the early 20th century

"I believe that awe-inspiring life-forms like whales can focus human minds on the urgency of ceasing our destruction of the wild world. Many of humanity's most intractable problems are caused by disregarding the voices of the Other—including non-humans."

– Roger Payne, *TIME* Magazine, June 2023

Watcher

Like a reef to the bow

I come upon them

On the wind-blasted hook of the Mullet, listening to the guide talk about stone types, the triangle of lighthouses, the now abandoned islands

the remains of the whaling station

jolt me from my stream of thought

thrown from the flow of my intentions into

the riptide of curiosity

The what?

What new discovery is this?

OF
IRON
AND
TIMBER

Lighthouse

North Mayo is more than a stretch away. Belting across the flat of it, towards slate blue mountains draped in cool white mist. It feels like another county altogether. The drive is well over an hour from my home near the county town. The slightly raised road winds through vast swathes of bogland. Every few miles, I spot a farmhouse blending into the hillside. I see no people.

Erris, *Iar Ros*, meaning western promontory. With the sea to the west and north, Nephin mountain to the east, it is set apart from the rest of the county.

Mayo is ancient. After the last Ice Age, Ireland was covered in deciduous and pine forest. These trees were felled during the Neolithic period. Without the trees, heavy rainfall washed nutrients from the soil, leaving it acidic. Dead organic matter would not decompose, which led to the formation of the blanket bogs which cover much of north Mayo. Not far from here are pre-bog field systems from the Mesolithic period, known as the Céide Fields. They contain a 1500-hectare archaeological site, the most expansive Stone Age monument in the world. The megalithic tombs that were built throughout the Neolithic period and into the Bronze Age can be found all over the county. This is where the first evidence of people in Mayo exists. It's the beginning. But that's not where I'm going today.

The lighthouse at Blacksod sneaks up on me, further away and then suddenly there. It is otherworldly in its desolation, especially at this time of year. Small fishing boats bob in the harbour. Men in yellow wax gear are unloading lobster pots from a trawler. We're tucked into the mouth of the bay here. On the map, the Mullet peninsula looks like a curling index finger, and Blacksod pier is the fingernail. The battered look about the boat and its commanders tells me they've been out much further – West, where the Atlantic is hell-deep and merciless.

Blacksod is unusual for a lighthouse. Granite and square, it looks more like a military bunker than a beacon of light. I'm here to write a poem. A man meets me and gives me a tour. I'm struck by how young he is, late twenties, possibly early thirties. It's normal, in isolated rural areas, to be met by teenagers working jobs before they leave for college, or those in late middle age who stayed and raised their families here. But my generation, the one with accessible education and birth control, were usually off elsewhere – in cities with job opportunities and all-night gyms, working in Australia or Canada, off seeking the Irish emigrant dream.

My guide tells me that he was indeed away, but he's been back a couple of years. His family is from the Mullet, and he loves it here. He mentions the quiet and the surfing culture.

It's a great buzz over the summer, he says.

I follow him up the steps to the small glass room of light that gives the building its name. The view is vast. I scan the water, a childish giddiness in me expecting to see a whale or submarine break the surface. To one side of the lighthouse, the harbour, but on the other it looks out across the bay, onto the ferry's routes out to the islands. Here, the stone lays in smooth, tiered slabs like an outdoor theatre. I ask my guide about using the location for a poetry performance, but he's quick to tell me that the waves come fast and sudden, sometimes hitting as high as where we are standing now.

In 1944, weather reports taken from this lighthouse caused Eisenhower to delay the Normandy landings. If the unexpected bad weather had hit as the landing crafts did, D-day may have had a different outcome.

Out here, on the edge of Europe, nothing beyond but thousands of miles of ocean.

Out here things can happen that change the course of everything.

And this is where my head is, the land, history, my own romance with the county. But the guide has moved on: a brief overview of the other lighthouses, the bay itself, points of note.

'Inishkea ...'

And I am half listening and half wrapped in my own thoughts.

'Remains of the whaling station ...'

The film

Back at home, I watch the film online. Soundless. The rise and fall of the boat. The men move jerkily, old-timey movie style, because that's what this is, an old movie, more than a hundred years old. But here it is. Real.

That this is here, our Mayo waters.

A quarter-century I've called this county home. Wriggled my toes in that same ocean. Stared out to where the grey water meets the grey sky, the strip of gold that splits the two. The ever-shifting light that casts the landscape into such uncertainty, so that a darkness could be cloud shadow, a forest, an unnoticed lake? You might wonder if you know the place at all.

The screen jolts.

A breaking of the surface, too smooth to be a wave. A spray. This huge creature. A man guides the harpoon.

Explosion.

The *tethered whale* blows.

Final breaths.

The greyscale boat follows

in its wake.

I hunch over my laptop. The room has grown darker as the summer rushes towards autumn. Outside, the clouds are tumbling like playful calves on the verge of butting heads. They roll in from over the sea, keeping the county wet and green.

Watching the blubber being stripped from the carcass. Flinching, or flensing. Strip by strip by strip. So exposed.

Oh, I know that feeling.

And so, it starts. This niggling, like a crush.

Submerged in fascination, in my object of desire.

Still from *Whaling Afloat and Ashore*, **Robert Paul (1908).**
Courtesy of the Irish Film Institute

These are the facts of it

'For nine years between 1908 and 1922, two UK-registered, Norwegian-owned whaling stations and a fleet of catcher vessels operated on the Mullet Peninsula in Co. Mayo; on Rusheen Island in the Inishkea Islands and at Ardelly Point near Blacksod. The Inishkea station (1908–1913) was owned by the Arranmore Whaling Company, while the Ardelly Point station (1910–1922) was owned by the Blacksod Whaling Company and later by the Norwegian Syndicate Akties Nordhavet.'[1]

The boats, known as whalers, were operated by Norwegians.

The stations employed local men.

Reports tell us 894 whales were killed. This figure doesn't account for the whales that were struck, died, and sank without being captured. Cetologist Conor Ryan estimates the number to be closer to a thousand.

This is the what, but I want to know the why.

Roots

I'm not from here. I moved to Mayo as a child when my parents left Dublin. I returned at various ages, for various reasons: 19, 24, 26. Money, usually, a need for space to write, poor mental health. I returned to live here permanently a few years ago.

To me, it has always felt like a place on the edge. A place people flee from and to. I don't know this land like I should. I'm a blow-in, to use the term for non-natives that move to the countryside, and now I've brought yet another blow-in with me.

He thinks of my life as here. In his mind, I am a Mayo woman.

'You are Mayo,' he said in one of his sappier moments, 'beautiful, unappreciated'.

I scoffed at him. I've known this place for a quarter of a century, and I had no idea of its whaling history. I had no idea of much of its history. I'd been too keen to look outward, to reach something, my eye always on an imagined horizon.

He's been in my life over a decade. Our attraction, the electric pursuit of my life. We bonded over a love of the sea. I loved its creatures, its romance. He, the ships, the adventure.

'My white whale,' I would joke, arms around his shoulders. A part of me liked to make him the prey.

Mayo is not mine, but I am of it. It is my home, and where I am raising my family. I am rooting myself here. It's this persistent need to know the place that brings me to the whales.

The riches of the sea

I start where I always do: research. I read and prove myself ignorant. It is a game I can't imagine growing bored with.

When I think of whales, I think of Arctic waters and *National Geographic*, but whales have long been a source of profit in Ireland, as they have worldwide. As far back as the medieval records of the Annals of Ulster, we can find reference to both stranded whales and to whaling. Under the year 828.3, we find 'a great slaughter of sea-hogs on the coast of Art Cianachta by foreigners'.[2]

Foreigners was one of the words used in the Annals to describe Vikings, perhaps the ancestors of those who would again hunt whales in Irish waters over a thousand years later.

Fishes Royal

                                   a shocking beast

                Swift-swimming monsters

Herring Hog

                          Immense monster

                  Sea-hog

Leviathan

                                         sea monster

                        devil of the deep[3]

The Senchus Mór, the early Irish legal text from the 8th century, says 'whatever thing is cast ashore in a territory, whether a crew of shipwrecked people, or a whale, the whole territory is bound to save it from the strand.'[4]

In July 1295, a Kerry lord, Robert de Clohulle, was charged with having appropriated a whale to his own use 'in prejudice of the Crown'. In reply, Robert refuted the charge, stating that by ancient custom in Ireland, 'such great whales are reported wreck of the sea', a right which his father had before him.[5]

Whales were more than a fascination. They were a resource. Something to be salvaged, like a shipwreck. A welcome to any coastal community.

In 1324, King Edward II enacted the Fishes Royal statute whereby 'the King shall have wreck of the sea throughout the realm, whales and great sturgeons in the sea or elsewhere within the realm, except in places privileged.'[6]

St Brendan holding mass on the back of a whale (1621).
Illustration by Wolfgang Kilian

Though from the 17th century, this image is illustrating a much older story. The immram of Saint Brendan, of which many varying manuscripts exist, tells the story of Brendan the Navigator (c. AD 484–c. 577), an early Irish monastic saint, sees him land on an island with his crew only to discover it is in fact a whale.

[1]

𝕾𝖙𝖗𝖆𝖓𝖌𝖊 & 𝖀𝖆𝖔𝖓𝖉𝖊𝖗𝖋𝖚𝖑 𝕹𝖊𝖜𝖘

FROM

IRELAND:
OF A

WHALE
OF

A Prodigious Size, being Eighty Two Foot long : Caſt Aſhore on the Third of this Inſtant *February*, near *DUBLIN* ; and there Expoſed to Publick View.

In a Letter to a Perſon of Quality.

SIR,

WE have had ſo many Prodigies of this Kind, that I wou'd not trouble you with any impertinent or improbable Relation, had not half the Kingdom, as well as my ſelf, been Eye-witneſſes to it. And I Queſtion not, but the thing being ſo generally known, and talk'd of, you will have Letters from ſeveral others this Poſt to confirm the Truth thereof.

In the County of *Lowth*, between *Dublin* and *Drohedah*, on the Third of this Inſtant *February*, was ſeen, about Eight of the Clock in the Morning, a Whale of the moſt Prodigious Size as ever had been ſeen in theſe parts of the World, appearing about a League off, like a moving Iſland, or a huge Black Caſtle in the midſt of the Ocean. When it came nearer the Shore, it ſeem'd like *Irelands*-Eye, the Hill of *Hoth*, or ſome vaſt Mountain upon the Sea-Coaſt ; the Sea, by the continual breaking of the Billows, (as if they diſdain'd to be Bounded by thoſe Banks) being all in a White Foam round about it.

In this plight the Prodigious *Leviathan* held Combat with the Floods for above Six Hours, as if he had challeng'd all the Sea-Gods to the Engagement, and been in Diſpute with *Neptune* for the Empire. Sometimes he was above, and ſometimes under the Waves, belching and throwing up ſuch vaſt Streams, and Spouts of Water out of his Mouth, as ſeem'd to put out the Sun, playing, like Water-Engins, againſt the Clouds, which accompany'd with ſmoak out of his Noſtrils, and frequent Flaſhes of Lightning from his Gaſtly Eyes, ſtruck Terror in the amazed Multitude, who by this time, from all parts round, were gathered upon the Sea-Coaſt, to ſee the Event of this ſo wonderful and terrible a Prodigy.

To hear the ſeveral Opinions, Fears and Conſternations, of the *Fingallians*, and *Monaghas*, Bred in ſome Pity, in others Laughter. To hear one calling for St. *Patrick*, another for St. *Dominick*, one for *Colomkill*, another for *Phelemback*, to Save them from the Fury of the great *Leviathan*, and the Terror of the Day of Judgment, which they were aſſured was at hand. To me it was pleaſure to Obſerve the variety of Paſtimes and Humours amongſt 'em ; ſome ſetting up the *Hullaloo*, and *Iriſh* Howl, others ſinging *Mackellamone* and the *Crone*, ſome at their *Ave-Maries*, others at the *Whip of Dunboin*, ſome at their *Padreens*, others at a Jig of *Balruddery*, and Dance of *Baldoile*. To ſee *Sheela* at her Prayers, and *Nabla* at her Sneezing, *Dermot* at his Beads, and *Rory* at his *Bolcane* and *Uſquebah* ; ſome run home to their Wives, others to the Father Confeſſor ; while many ſtay'd, ſome out of hopes of Prey, others out of Curioſity, to ſee the Reſult of it.

About

About Two a Clock the Tyde going out, he was left like a great Ship on ground, with the Keel upwards, half way in Mud and Water, still strugling and spouting out Water in vast quantities, which being carried by an Easterly Wind, sometimes reach'd as far as the Shore.

About an hour after he was left upon the Strand, wallowing in the Mud, beating the ground with his Head, and flapping with his Tail, in such violent and hideous manner, that the Wind thereof blew away several People, who came running down upon the Strand, Roaring as if there had been a Legion of Dutch Cannon within him, and with that dreadful and horrible Noise, as if they had been Discharged at the Broad-side, for his last Volley. In this Hurricane there was not a Cabbin in Seven Miles round that had a Glass Window left upon it, all their Drink was soured, and their Milk turn'd into Curds and Whey.

In this fury, *Leviathan* expired, when the Assembly taking fresh Courage by his Death, laid Siege to the deserted Garrison. Engines are erected, and he is brought ashore, being in length Eighty Two Foot, the Tongue weighing above Six Hundred Pound, as soft, but much bigger than a Feather-Bed. The Heart bigger and fatter than the Body of a great Ox, the Ribs and Bones like Beams, and the Teeth all Whale-bone, like the Rafters of a House meeting in Couples, but something closer, with white Beards like Wheat-Sheafs at the end of them, and the Tail like a chequer'd stript Scotch Plad, split in the middle, and spreading open on both sides. In the Mouth of which, being propt up with the mast of a *Dublin Gibbard*, many People have been together.

In the opening of him they found Three Men and a Boy, with Three large Horns of Snuff, and a Runlet of *Usquebah*. The Men were known, being poor Fisher-Men belonging to a Creek within Four Miles of *Droheda*. One of the Men having an Oar in his Hand which struck fast in his Gills, and the Boat running a drift, stuck cross in his Throat, which was thought to be the occasion of his wreck. Others finding a quantity of Barrel-staves within him, thought it might be with excess of some hot Liquors which agreed not with his Phlegmatick Constitution.

In the dissecting of him, the Meat which is yet to be seen, being rather Flesh than Fish, the Skin and upper Parts resembing fatted-smoakt-Bacon, and under that, red Flesh, like swill'd Mutton or Dutch Beef, of which many have Eaten, and found it so.

The Head, Heart, Tail, and other Parts are yet to be seen in *Oxmontown* in *Dublin*, as you will find by the Bills, which are Printed and given out in this City, which I have sent you Inclosed.

A Copy of the Bills as they are Printed and given out in *Dublin*.

At the WHITE-HOUSE in the midst of *St. Mary's-Lane*, in *Oxmontown* in *Dublin*, is to be seen,

The Head, Heart, Tail, and other Parts of the most Prodigious and Monstrous WHALE, that ever was seen or heard of in these Parts of the World, being in length Eighty Two Foot, &c.

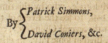

By ⎨ *Patrick Simmons,*
      David Coniers, &c.

Price Half a Cobb.

LONDON, Printed for S. *Kemp*. 1683.

'Strange and Wonderful News from Ireland: Of a Whale of a Prodigious Size, Being Eighty Two Foot Long, Cast Ashore on the Third of This Instant February, Near Dublin, and There Exposed to Publick View.'
Courtesy of the National Library of Ireland

The Norwegians were not the first to set up a whaling business in Ireland. In 1737, a Lieutenant Samuel Chaplain, having heard reports of an abundance of whales in Donegal, petitioned the Irish parliament for funding for the venture. He argued that it would be 'a national account' that would provide 'a commodity of Bone and Oil of Exportation', and that there were 'a great Number of able sailors, who may be employed in other Seasons to fish for Pilchards, Cod, Ling and Herring etc. in the same vessels.' He secured £500, but died before he could collect the money.[7]

In the 1760s, Thomas Nesbitt purchased a ship fit for whaling. He was a Donegal man whose family was involved in the fisheries. He even developed a gun harpoon a century before they were widely in use. He petitioned the House of Commons for financial assistance to construct a shore-based station. The station was built in Port, Donegal, and had some success.

Though the likely cause of the dissolution of the station was economic, a more dramatic conclusion was reported in James McParlan's *Statistical Survey of County Donegal*. 'One of the whales... angry at this invasion of their empire of the ocean, gave Mr Nisbett's boat a whisk of its tail, and shattered it in pieces; two men were lost... this accident put an end to his whale fishery.'[8]

Sea hog

I source a book about the Mayo stations, *Irish Whales and Whaling* by Dr James Fairley. It's out of print, and I pay half a week's shopping bill to have a secondhand copy shipped from America. I read it until my eyes start to scratch and ache.

'The very size of these animals is a direct consequence of their having taken to water.'[9]

I go for a swim. I prefer the sea. Fat women look better in the sea. In the gym pool, we look like we're making too much of an effort.

I watch my skin below the water. Mottle green. Nail beds purple. The cold water is changing my blood flow, and the refraction of light through the surface warps what I am seeing. In the water, the body is a different beast.

Beached whales can die from their own weight. The bulk. The drag.

I hid my body for years. Large breasts, larger attitude. An easy target. Slow-moving and overly familiar. The undulating land of my body functioned as ornament, object. Better to fold it away, in on itself.

Only growing a person, feeding them with my milk, did I learn of my own utility.

I swim to strengthen my muscles. To feel light, like there might be a world where I am strong, untethered.

Back on the computer, among articles and archives, I read and reread.

Monstrous fury
of the great leviathan

in the opening of him
they found Three Men and a Boy

angry at this invasion

What is it that makes the men hunt them? Where, in the whale, cries *Come, I am here for the taking, my existence is for you, and when I flee you, it is an insult?*

Maybe, again, I am projecting.

Perhaps *my* mariner will understand. His sympathies lie where mine can't. He feels the legacy of the working man, the seafarer, the father, the provider. He knows the masculine urge to hunt.

At heart, I'm still a child naming the calves in the fields. I stomp on the brakes to let a pheasant cross the road. All the mouse traps in our house are humane. I have always identified more with the prey.

So, I ask him. *Explain it to me.*

Tráigha

Sing the song they never sang of us.
    Have the Atlantean air ring with sun-
sweetened swells, profundo drone.
    Make your accompaniment little more
than a seasoning of wind, froth-spewing
    breakers, salty peninsula air piping
like a shanty through drystone ruins
    that cling, barnacle-keen, to the machair.
Harmonise to the creak and moan
    of timbers, surf-seethe, cormorant caw,
a ship's bell faintly clanging
    and, for the sharp-eared, reach
your crescendo with the low-pitched, undersea
    echoes of humpback whales
reverberating through the fathoms.

Wetten your throats, rinse the song clean:

What spurs the hunt?

To Hell or to Connacht

The Mullet peninsula and the Inishkea islands are in the Barony of Erris. On our way to the pier, we drive through the village of Binghamstown. Barony. Bingham. The words clash against the landscape. Perhaps how untouched the place seems makes its colonial leftovers more obvious.

The Cromwellian settlement displaced native Irish families from eastern and southern parts of the country to the less valued land west of the Shannon. The land was divided and subdivided as huge estates were granted to the Commonwealth soldiers. The bloody years of Cromwell are well documented. They have seeped into the psyche of Ireland.

The famine of 1845–52 hit Mayo hard. Nearly 90 percent of the population were dependent on the potato. Evictions increased, aided by the Gregory clause in the Poor Law Extension Act 1847 which excluded relief from anyone who had more than a quarter acre, forcing people to give up their land to survive. People died and emigrated in their thousands. Workhouses built in the early 1840s were located in Ballina, Ballinrobe, Belmullet, Castlebar, Claremorris, Killala, Newport, Swinford and Westport. Famine graves, lazy-beds, deserted villages; reminders laid into the dirt.

The land agitation was started in Mayo in 1879 by Michael Davitt, James Daly and others. It brought the greatest social change Ireland had seen. The meeting in Irishtown arose out of a threat to evict tenants for arrears of rent from a local absentee landlord. Davitt later met Fenian leader John Devoy and Charles Stewart Parnell and agreed on a 'new departure' where Fenians and constitutional nationalists combined efforts to reform the Irish land system. Parnell urged tenants at a meeting in Westport to 'hold a firm grip on your homesteads and lands'. The National Land League of Mayo was founded in Castlebar by Davitt, and within two months the campaign became national.

The Land War over the next two decades took place across the country. It was resolved by a scheme of state-aided land purchase. Tenant farmers became owner-occupiers within a generation. The land agitation paved the way for the rebellion, which led to Independence.

After Independence, Mayo, like the rest of the country, saw high birth rates and few opportunities for employment. Emigration was high, especially among the educated (the so-called 'brain drain') and with more opportunities for education, Mayo was left with an ageing population. Farming was the chief source of livelihood in Mayo for the early and mid-20th century, though fewer children stayed to farm family land and increased industrial-isation of farming practices has had catastrophic consequences on farmers and land alike.

It was the blanket bog that provided much employment in Erris post-inde-pendence. In the 1950s, state company Bord na Móna purchased 20,000 acres of bogland in the area, and the Electricity Supply Board built a peat-powered electricity generation station at Bellacorrick.

North Mayo has not benefited from much of the flourishing of other parts of the county. It is inaccessible by rail, served from the county town by the R313, a route which has not been updated in any significant way since its installation in 1824. The poor infrastructure makes it unattractive for busi-ness investment, and employment opportunities are limited, but the roads are not the only route. The sea off Erris has more than once been a source of interest for foreign business.

Barbarous people

> *commit whoredom, hold no wedlock, ravish, steal and commit all abomination without scruple of conscience*

atheists or infidels

> *Great force must be the instrument but famine must be the means, for till Ireland be famished it cannot be subdued.*

As filthy as the swine[10]

The islands

I go to the history books to find out about Inishkea. A problem I come across is perception. Many who wrote about Inishkea while it was inhabited were travel writers with colonial mindsets, such as Alexander Innes Shand, who in 1884 wrote:

> 'Inishkea, where the people form an independent state of their own and must be pretty nearly heathens. They acknowledge no landlord, they pay no rates, they elect a monarch of their own and though a priest does come at intervals to confess, to marry or to christen them, they have an idol they regularly worship and propitiate before their boats put out to sea.'[11]

When there was no one living on the island writing and publishing books with a more accurate account of life, the eye of the outsider, and the bias they bring with them, gets remembered as fact. Relying on books alone won't do for me this time.

'I'm a blow-in,' I explain to anyone I ask to talk to me about the whales. I'm afraid of being seen as an outsider set on exploiting the story of a place I'm not from. Cultural appropriation of a different parish.

Two people we interview use the same turn of phrase to ease my concerns.

'We all blew in from somewhere.'

The truth of this becomes evident to me as I research the islands further. The islands of Inishkea, named after Saint Cé, lie 3km off the coast of the Mullet. The islands were often portrayed as being a kind of pagan enclave isolated by the ocean. While there's evidence of pre-Christian settlements on the islands, there was not one continuous population isolated from the mainland. The last settlement of Inishkea started in the 1760s. Families came from the Mayo coast, the first man being Dan McGinty, sent there by the landlord in Newport House. Many of those families had come to Mayo from Ulster after the Irish rebellion of 1641. We all blew in from somewhere indeed.

One man we visit is a descendent of Dan McGinty. Tomás Bán Ó Raghallaigh now lives in Ballina, and has written extensively on the topic of Inishkea:

> I was always known as Tomás Bán or Tommy Bán. Because not

alone I had blonde hair, but my family were known as the Báns. Seán Bán was my great-grandfather, and the Reillys go back generations on the island, mostly on the north island. My mother was McGinty, and they were the first settlers on Inishkea in the 1760s. I remember reading a record in Castlebar Jail, in 1741, about 100 years before the famine, there was a big freeze. Thousands died in Ireland and everywhere in a lot of Europe. Forty Inishkea men were jailed for piracy in the Castlebar jail. Now that means there was a settlement on the island in 1741. But it was empty by 1765 when Dan McGinty went to it.

Griffith's Valuation in 1855 records 35 families on Inishkea South. The islanders made their living through farming, fishing, and the sale of kelp and poitín. They lived outside the law to some extent, selling poitín, not paying their rent or taxes. Rate collectors refused to go to the island because they would be stoned from their boats. The islanders traded with mainlanders, the islands being a perfect setting for poitín-making as it was so difficult for strangers, such as excise officers, to approach. According to Rita Nolan's *Within the Mullet*, clergymen and the police were among the best customers.

Tomás tells me the poitín made on the island was called Uisce Cé:

> Maxwell [the writer] said the famous Boycott's wife would drink nothing else. The government didn't have much head on Inishkea, you know, the landlord held the rent at that time. There were more poitín raids than raids. There was actually excise police on Inishkea. They had to put a barracks on it. They were revenue police to put a stop to the poitín. Some people were even objecting to councils when the women used to come out to have their babies in Belmullet Hospital. Oh, the bloody Inishkeas shouldn't be let in because they're not paying their taxes.

Island communities lived with a degree of self-sufficiency in a country where exportation of grain and high rates had led to famine not even a century previously. It was pre-independence Ireland. For centuries, people had been driven further and further west for the chance of making any living at all. After island living, the next stop was America, an option which many did take. While mainland Mayo was decimated by the famine, the Inishkea islands' population increased. Piracy is one explanation for this, hijacking sailing ships from their currachs, using stones to drive the crew below deck. To live inside the law increased your chance of not living at all. While mainlanders died in their thousands, the islanders survived.

While each island did have its own *rí*, the idea that they were pagans or heretics is outdated. Nolan notes that 'the people of Inishkea were no more heathen than their neighbours in the Mullet or throughout Ireland. Religion here at the that time was a strange mixture of Catholic worship and old pagan customs and superstition.'[12]

The islands provided little except trouble to the landlord, Edward Walshe, and he sold them to the Congested Districts Board (CDB) in 1907. The CDB was set up by the government in 1891 to 'investigate the lamentable social and economic conditions prevailing in much of the west of Ireland, and to do what it could to ameliorate them by buying over land, building roads, bridges and harbours, and by encouraging agriculture, cottage-industries and the fisheries.'[13]

This promised new prosperity to the islanders. Early in 1908, the CDB sold a 4½-acre site on Rusheen, a tidal islet off Inishkea South, to the Arranmore Whaling Company for £100.

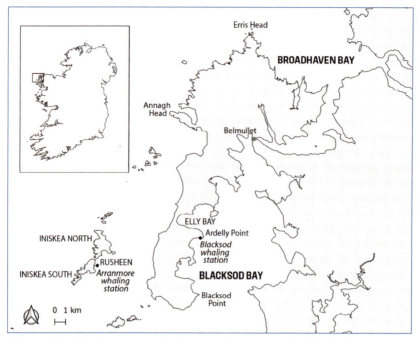

Map of the Mullet peninsula showing location of both whaling stations.

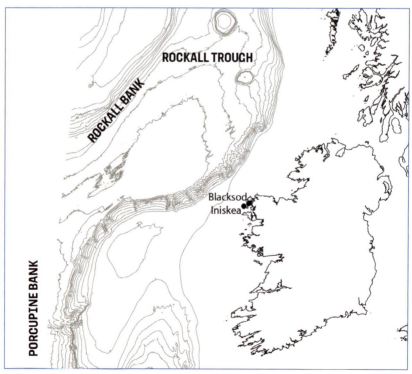

Map of Ireland showing proximity of the stations to the deep waters of Rockall Trough. Maps: Éadaoin Ní Néill

Watcher as day-tripper

I have to see it. Where this happened. Mariner is happy for the excuse to be seabound.

Our guides are descendants of the last islanders. Their boat takes the waves at speed, kicking up spray. Two dolphins pass, breaking the surface briefly.

We watch the water like we're waiting

for attack. The unrelenting ruptures in the black.

Spears of spray. The toil and tumble of currents

or something just below the surface.

Gulls wheel above us, shrieking like we're harbingers

of fish to come. Waiting for water to colour like syrupy merlot.

At low tide, Rusheen, where the station was located, can be accessed by foot from Inishkea South. Our guide eyes the sea.

'The tide is on the way in. You might have time.'

He doesn't recommend it, but we've come a long way and the boats will soon go into storage for the winter. This is our only shot.

We clamber over the rocks and sand and onto Rusheen. It can't take more than three or four minutes. We hunker on the grass, running our hands over rusted remnants. We know little to nothing. It's guesswork. The cylinders turned to scrap metal. We frame the place, try to stick it in our minds to return to, when we know more.

It feels like being at the scene of mass murder. I am reminded of the chill I felt at other jaunts to sites of historical significance, battlefields and war camps. But of course, it wasn't murder. It was business. There's a difference. Can an animal be murdered, or does such a grave allegation belong to an act committed against humans? Consideration of mammals as equal to humans has more than once landed me in trouble with those who find it insulting. The tide is coming in.

'Come on,' says Mariner, 'before it gets too deep.'

I'm reluctant to leave, but already the stones we clambered over have disappeared below the water. It's impossible to see how deep it is, but it looks only to be a few inches. Mariner starts to wade across in his boots. Quickly the water is reaching his jeans, but he's too stubborn to turn back, Jack Sparrow in denim.

I hitch up my skirt. My sandals are sea-friendly. The water's coolness on a day as hot as today is a relief. We land on the main island giggling. Our exasperated guide lends Mariner some wax fishing overalls. I snap a photograph of him among the ruins. He looks like he's just fallen off a trawler.

We take a stroll over the far side of the island and find a small beach. There's no one else on it, there being only the ten or so people from our boat on the entire island. I swim in togs anyway. The horizon is hazy and impossibly far away. The air is so hot that the shallow water of the bay is balmy. Mariner dips and dives like a shag.

While we wait for the ferry, I sit on the pier and look for fish. The water sparkles in the afternoon summer sun, deep and clear as a pool. The odd shoal of small translucent fish dart by. I want to jump in, but I'm dry and the boat's on its way. There's a seal bobbing in the harbour, close to the shore. There's only ever a boat or two out here. On the land, even on an island as remote as this, sheep have ravaged most of the biodiversity. At least in the water, there are fewer signs of human interference, but its clarity serves to show its emptiness.

It's the same across huge swathes of Mayo. Mountainside and bogland. The absence of industry, of streetlamps, of cars, of plastic bottles, leads us to believe we're in the wilderness, but the emptiness is not natural. This land of little commercial value is still used for grazing sheep. Sitka spruce plantations that allow little other life to grow. It's a postcard version of wildness. A distraction from how barren our land has become.

On the ferry back the waves kick up, soaking my extremities. The wind dries them almost immediately, leaving behind a crust of salt. I hold my fingertips to Mariner's lips. He licks them.

Cottages on Inishkea South. Image: Paul Kinsella (2023)

Rusheen. Image: Paul Kinsella (2023)

Inishkea South to Rusheen at low tide. Image: Paul Kinsella (2023)

Remnants on Rusheen. Images: Paul Kinsella (2023)

Remnants on Rusheen. Images: Paul Kinsella (2023)

View of Inishkea South from Rusheen. Image: Paul Kinsella (2023)

Tryworks foundations on Rusheen. Image: Paul Kinsella (2023)

A little about the whales
(as they knew them)

What we know about whales is increasing all the time. By the early 20th century, the image of the giant predatory fish was long gone. Whales belong to a group of marine mammals called cetaceans. Cetaceans fall into two categories: toothed whales and baleen whales.

Toothed whales include dolphins, porpoises, and the only of the toothed whales to be considered one of the great whales: the sperm whale. Baleen whales are named for the fibrous comb-like material they have in the place of teeth. To whalers, baleen was known as whalebone. Baleen whales are further divided into rorquals, right whales, and grey whales. The right whales are slow, shore-hugging animals, named for being the 'right' whale to catch as they float after death.

Of the whales caught at the Mayo stations, most were rorquals, with the exception of right whales in the early years and sperm whales when the boats went further from shore.

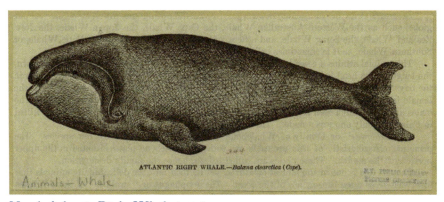

ATLANTIC RIGHT WHALE.—*Balæna cisarctica* (*Cope*).

North Atlantic Right Whale (1885)

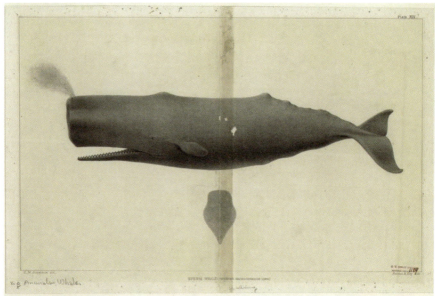

Sperm whale (1874)

Finback (1874)

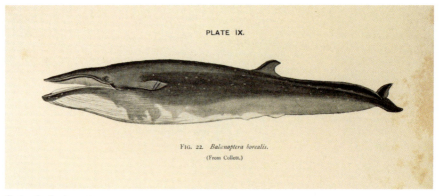

Sei whale (1900)

HUMPBACK WHALE (*Megaptera longimana* or *M. böops*), the representative of a genus of whalebone whales distinguished by the great length of the flippers. This whale (or a closely

Humpback Whale (*Megaptera longimana* or *böops*).

allied species) is found in nearly all seas; and when full-grown may reach from 45 ft. to 50 ft. in length, the flippers which are indented along their edges measuring from 10 ft. to 12 ft. or more. The general colour is black, but there are often white markings on the under surface; and the flippers may be entirely white, or parti-coloured like the body. Deep longitudinal furrows, folds or plaits occur on the throat and chest. It is said that the popular name refers to a prominence on which the back fin is set; but this " hump " varies greatly in size in different individuals. The humpback is a coast whale, irregular in its movements, sometimes found in " schools," at others singly. The whalebone is short, broad and coarse; but the yield of oil from a single whale has been as much as 75 barrels. A few examples of this whale have been taken in Scotland and the north of England (see CETACEA).

took a ｐ
beth's v
gown ar

chapel,
portrait
　Hump
subjects.
Bishop J
to the e
against t
per vario
　See B
*Athenae
Index to*
1547–15
Collier's
Biog.
　HUM
soldier
of Nov

Humpback whale (1911)

Blue whale (1920)

Weight

I'm reading everything about the whales I can find. One of the blue whales caught early on in industrial whaling weighed 136 tonnes. The accuracy of this is questionable as it was far too large to be weighed in one go and had to be severed into chunks.

This bond doth give thee here no jot of blood.[14]

What margins

        spilled

across the wood,   spattered onto faces,   clothes.

Scraps

      of blubber

        torn away

           by gulls.

I think of the weight of the soul in the debunked experiment: 21 grams.

The experiment was looking for proof, but all people really want is hope.

That there's a sliver of it in the *something*
which slips away when we're deconstructed to a sum of our parts.

A brief history of whaling

Subsistence whaling by indigenous communities went on for thousands of years. There's evidence of whales being hunted by harpoon as early as 6000 BCE.

Commercial whaling began in the 11th century with the Basques in the Bay of Biscay. They are thought to have learned their whaling techniques from the Vikings that plundered Basque country in 844 BCE. The industry grew and the abundance of whales across the ocean brought Basque fishermen to colonise North America.

In many ways, the history of whaling is entwined with the history of colonialism. In the 16th century, English, Dutch, and German industries were also whaling. By the 1650s, American whaling had begun.

Commercial whaling was based on sailing boats, rowboats, and the harpoon. Whales were chased and killed by a hand-thrown harpoon. The fast-swimming rorquals were rarely caught as they were both too fast and sank once killed.

Whale oil was the prime product, used as a light source and industrial lubricant. Baleen, or whalebone, was also valuable, especially before the development of plastic. Spermaceti, a thick substance from the head of a sperm whale which was solid at room temperature, was used in the making of candles.

As stocks closer to shore declined, whalers went further afield to find their prey. Whaling voyages could last years. Those on board were paid by lays, meaning their share of the profits. It was a gamble as no pay was certain, but it also meant that the more whales they caught, the more everyone on board earned. The whalemen were invested in the hunt. As we know, the whale was considered fishes royal and the crown demanded tax on the profit. Whalers were some of the earliest objectors to taxation without representation.

In whaling, we see the history of globalisation. *Moby Dick* has been called the great American novel. It is a novel not just about a whaling expedition, but about the American dream. Commercial whaling was early capitalism. Whaleships had owners, investors, captains, crew. Profits were invested in other industries or back into whaling. New Bedford, the heart of American whaling, is known as the city that lit the world.

The US was at the forefront of the whaling industry, peaking in the mid-19th century. When civil war broke out, many of the ships were used for war, and many did not emerge in one piece. The cost and recovery meant that after the war, whaling could not recommence swiftly, but in 1859, something happened which would change the course of whaling as an industry. It would, in fact, change the course of humanity.

GRAND BALL GIVEN BY THE WHALES IN HONOR OF THE DISCOVERY OF THE OIL WELLS IN PENNSYLVANIA.

Grand ball given by the whales in honor of the discovery of the oil wells in Pennsylvania. *Image: Vanity Fair* (1861)

When oil was discovered in Pennsylvania in 1859, there was a shift westward in the US economy. Here was a cheaper, safer and more available resource than whale oil. America moved away from whaling, but countries like Norway did not have the alternatives in the economy that the US did. Norway's own oil resources had not yet been discovered.

The industrial revolution was in full swing, and there was an increase in the use of coal. Steamships transformed the industry as they could keep up with the rorquals. With stocks of right and sperm whales low, plus less competition from the US, the limited supply meant the prices for whale oil remained profitable.

In addition to this, a complete system for killing rorquals was developed by Norwegian Sven Foyn in the 1860s. It consisted of a steamer ship, a cannon on the bow which fired an iron harpoon with exploding tip, and barbs which would open on impact, embedding themselves in the flesh of the whale and allowing the crew to haul the sinking body to the surface with an onboard winch. The carcass was then lanced and inflated with compressed air from the engines and towed back to shore.

These new technologies made it easier and faster to catch more whales. Profits increased and risk decreased. Other countries began to up their game, the UK developing a large fleet and leading expeditions to the southern oceans.

Depletion of stocks was an ongoing issue for all whalers. Moratoriums happened in national waters, which led whalers further and further afield.

death struggle,

the whale raced   breaking the water into miniature "seas"

spouting   aloft torrents of blood and vapour.

the fish   the vessel

no longer relied   on her engines

towed by   **her maddened capture,**

THE STATIONS

In 1904, the Norwegian Government implemented a 10-year ban in territorial waters. Stocks were depleted, and there had been protests from fisheries that whaling was harming their industry. The Norwegian whalers needed to go further afield to continue their business. This led them to Ireland.

While in the first year the whales were caught within ten miles of the coast, 'first-hand accounts from whalers indicate that catcher vessels would often leave in the evening and be on the whaling grounds by dawn. Assuming this was sunset to sunrise in mid-summer and steaming at 10 knots, the whaling ground was c.70 nautical miles (130 km) offshore.'[15]

This places the whaling grounds after the first year in the waters of Rockall trough. This is where deep diving species such as sperm whales were found. Humpback whales were already overexploited by commercial whaling, and few were caught in Mayo.

In both stations, the first catch was a Nordcapper (North Atlantic right whale). By the third season, no more right whales were caught. Today, the eastern North Atlantic right whale is thought to be functionally extinct due to the effects of commercial whaling.

Fin whales were by far the most abundantly taken. Perhaps surprisingly, more than 100 blue whales were also caught. The waters of Mayo were home to the largest animal to have ever existed.

Table of catches by species for Arranmore and Blacksod stations combined [16]

Year	Blue whale	Finback whale	Hump-back	Right	Sei	Sperm	Total
1908	19	21	1	5	31	0	77
1909	27	56	0	5	9	5	102
1910	12	51	3	8	39	7	120
1911	10	109	0	0	02	9	130
1912	8	38	0	0	4	10	60
1913	10	88	2	0	1	13	114
1914	13	70	0	0	2	4	89
1920	9	101	0	0	3	12	125
1922	18	56	0	0	0	3	77
TOTAL	126	590	6	18	91	63	894

Sons of sea rovers

By training and tradition, the hardy Norseman has always held premier place in the exciting adventure of whale fishing, and to this day he holds control. The chief shareholders even of the Irish companies are Norwegians, and the crews of the steamers which pursue the industry are recruited from the descendants of the Northern Sea rovers who conquered Britain, and worried the Irish kings 'til their final defeat at Clontarf in 1014. When these stations were first established, great expectations of employment were formed by the people of the Western coast, but their hopes could not be fulfilled, as the whale, like the bison and the buffalo, is becoming an extinct species because of its great worth to man.[17]

Immram Miolbhádorí

Hron-Rād

'sá hon vítt ok of vítt of veröld hverja?'[18]
(she... spoke with wisdom of all the worlds)

– Völuspá

We rise from our bunks in oilskins, breaths uncoiling
in knife-cool air along the predawn quay. We
huddle, smoking our pipes while the Atlantic stirs

to a musk of oakum. Diesel leaks from bilges to brine
in a lone, slick cataract as swells surge to surface.
The island is all hush, all shaded crags.

Foc's'le lamps glower as coffee brews in the galley,
a pot spewing steam like fjord mist. The *Bruun,*
sleek bellwether of the Oslo shipyards, is tethered

to a rolling undertow, gunwales damp as if payed
in shark blood, her harpoon gun slewing eight
feet aft and hinged in brass, savage shimmer.

At Skipper's brisk command, we get to work, hoist gear
aboard, wrestle with winches and stow harpoons;
a two-man job, metallic sheen braced with cold accord.

At first glance, gunner's pride mirrors their prey from head
to heel: barbs in brute mimicry of fins, midrib like its intended
victim's tail, four-edged, double-edged, flaring save

for the absence of flukes. We'd be well underway by now
if we moved as fluidly as the tides, at ease even amidst
rusting levers, ruptured crankshafts, half-coiled anchor

chains, leaning our collective ear to the waves'
whisper. Men grip the thwart for balance.
We slacken steel moorings, our berth a snarl

of dripping hawsers. The *Bruun* shoves surf aside
as smoke dances confusedly from her stack. The wake
churns, broadening abaft like ragged lace.

And we'll hunt them to the drowning of the world
Hunt them to the drowning of the world
We'll track them to the drowning of the world
Far, far beyond the grey whale-road

Joseph Brennan Album B, 1900.
Courtesy of the National Library of Ireland

Hvala Blástr

The horizon is like a shaving cut as daybreak
kindles to a cold blush from its crimson incision.
We lose sight of land, our world now

a chop shop of winches and cables, rudders, boilers
and bulk cargo handling. We cough a hymn to the sea
and the giants lurking in their abyssal Asgard.

The ship is a mere fragment in infinity
as we advance on the feeding grounds of our
behemoth prey, fit to dwarf us with a single breach.

Skin-eyed, the lookout scours the surge.
Headway is slow. We sail across miles and years
as if in escort, our ancestors and theirs

who marauded here once, bone-soaked wanderers
of the whale-road. A Gael's leathery skin-boat, scudding
coastal drift, pebble-eyed rowers who worshipped survival,

the first of us to berth this ebb: Dane rovers
or Norse sea-thieves reaping the fathom of winter
with atgeir-lance, a rash of longships speckling Hibernian waters,

clinker ribs reef-scathed, oars biting through the tide's
grey mirl. They, too, speared the basking titans —
whale blood has a scent only hunters can detect.

Warnings come as fair as the wind: "Ga ån!"
bellows through the brass trumpet. Skipper's
spitfire lingo mutes as he swivels the gun

back to dead reckoning, its pointed eye trained
through a flurry of petrels in circling riot
to a silver geyser. Frenzy on deck as all hands

see it for themselves. Flukes dissect the horizon.
Not a league off the starboard bow, in the grip
of the waves, we watch it rise: head like an anvil,

fizz of a brief plume, the finner's lithe shadow glides,
a snowy underbelly in a spurt to a scud. Skipper
stands restive at the gun platform, clay pipe clamped

at his lower lip, eye luminous as an ill-gotten pearl.

                              *

For such a scene will be witnessed eternally,
whalers ample as oil spill — over this elemental vista
we shellbacks pursued the pods. A swarm of cachalot

gored by Basque keel's keen cut, or the Dutch at Spitsbergen,
steadfast in their pursuit, lambency of their lanterns
to ignite a rare golden age for the Yankee will, as iron

as their lances. English steam and steel on course
through a saga of blood. We, too, sail on that hallowed rite
of passage to industry's thunderous drum, tonnage

of the hunt, knives rinsed clean of viscera in a galley sink.
We taste again the burnt tang of naphtha Nantucketian flame,
floes echoing restlessly, noble knaves of the flensing barb

when we used mere oars and canvas on a hunt, as Ostmen,
as Romans, in oilskin or pelt, cordage-creek or gliding steady,
from crow's nest to bilge, trusting in the try-works' art

even as our luck turned laggard, even as the earth is disinherited
by cartographers, lest we ever forget the proximate sea from
which our survival was ever plucked. We sail to the giant

dead ahead, iron shafts gripped to puncture his godly rib.

We'll range and we'll rove
'Way from shelter and stove,
Far from harbour and cove
'Til a prize is struck
For a gale is thundering
And the brine is sundering
Lubbers call it wandering
But we call it work

Harpoon head from Inishkea.

Artefact courtesy of Turas Siar.

Image: Paul Kinsella

Mél-regn

The harpoon strafes forward with a roar that mangles the calm. A bolt gashing a cream line through azure, a darting iron that blooms to lodge in the vast flesh. Even as blood spasms from the blowhole, the beast will not die. A finner is no nordcapper; it will not swim contentedly to the slaughter. It goes on in fitful lurches, pillowed jaw no longer unhinging for a glut of krill, but clamped in forward trajectory as it tows us like an angry dog. The harpoon's shaft is embedded in the dark gash. As the gun is reloaded, the beast slows as if submitting to its fate, but again breaks the surface with its tail like an anchor silhouetted against the crisp headway where sky meets sea. It swings down like some colossal mallet, crashing flatly on our prow, moulting barnacles and trailing crested froth. Vibrations judder the hull, jolting us fore-and-aft. Skipper's harpoon fires ahead, full-bore rumble with the cable uncoiling wildly, the winch gnashing and, all through the runnings, deckhands young and old eye the line's arc like confessors. Fatal drill finds its grip between fin and eye, the cruellest kiss devised, water lapping off its bulk. Even in death-thrash, no denying its splendour. The sea is paved with a hush so abrupt even the birds suspend their cries. Some toppled dignity remains in the beast's brine-glazed eye. This kill is a victory, a testament to our industry, blood in the water fragrant with oil. The winch hisses the rope back, draws the driftwood-dark carcass to the vessel's bow, and lashes the greyscale bulk to starboard. We hack the flukes away so as not to slow our progress, returning their worthless grizzle to the deep. Tube-drawn air from the belly of the boat inflates the carcass as if it were already swelling with rot, ensuring it bobs alongside the *Bruun*. Precious cargo pressed against the hull, held fast by chain alone. Skipper retakes the helm, his hands still dripping, and sets a weighted course east. The engines roar as if in triumph, steaming back at the slowest pace to the island moorings in the calm that follows carnage, a current of red unspooling in our wake.

SS Carsten Bruun arrives with a whale.
Image: Leslie Hamilton Wilson, courtesy of the Johnson Museum

Arranmore Whaling Company
These Poor Islands

The Arranmore Whaling Company is a deceptive name considering it operated on Inishkea. It was named for the island in Donegal on which the station was initially planned, but there was resistance among the locals. There had already been stations set up in Scotland, and there was a widespread belief that whaling damaged fisheries and was a public hygiene hazard. According to Fairley, 'The civil disturbances in Norway and disquiet among Shetlanders had been well publicised: astonishment rapidly changed to apprehension and indignation and before long there was a solid core of resistance. Some of the gentry, judging from subsequent developments, simply resented the prospect of foreigners coming in to make money under their noses.'[12]

The Government Fisheries Branch held an enquiry, and the company was not granted a permit. Within mere weeks, the site on Inishkea had been secured. It is thought to be due to the manoeuvres of the naturalist Reverend William Spotswood Greene, who was a member of the CDB and Inspector of Fisheries. These positions meant he knew that the fisheries-related objections of whaling weren't accurate, and as a member of CDB he was keen to bring a significant source of employment to somewhere as remote as Inishkea.

There was no legislation to deal with whaling in Ireland. The Fisheries Branch brought in bylaws to regulate whaling. Whales could not be taken within three miles of the coast or further north than Downpatrick Head.

Tomás Bán explains:

> The CDB didn't consult the islanders, and there was hostility first. The building started and the employment started then, and they mellowed a bit. But if the Norwegians thought they were going to get the Inishkeas nice and easy, they were soon to learn otherwise. Because the Inishkeas never worked for anyone. They were very independent. They were self-employed. They fished, they farmed, and their living was mostly made on the sea and produced from the sea, you know, from everything from kelp to winkles. And then they'd go out and do the lobster and craws, which no one else was doing.

The station included a slipway, sheds with boilers and dryers, a forge, living quarters, administration building, and a firehouse. LM Christensen and Erling Lund were the chief shareholders of the whaling company. There were two whaling steamers called *Erling* and the *Carsten Bruun*, the latter being owned by Lorentz Bruun, a shareholder who would later leave to set up his own whaling company in Blacksod.

The islanders were said to allow only men from the south island to work at the station. The Norwegian men worked and slept on the ships. The islanders worked at cooperage and the forge, and in the processing of the whales. The Norwegians, at least at first, flensed the whales (stripped it of the blubber) as this was a skilled job. However, Pat O'Reilly learned the skill and was later employed at the station in Blacksod.

At the time, Johnny O'Donnell was the *rí* of Inishkea South. He came from Roundstone for the fishing, and he stayed and married an Inishkea woman. He spoke both English and Irish and could act as an interlocutor between the workers and the foreman at the station. Richard Walsh who worked on the Inishkea station for three years reported that several islanders eventually picked up bits of Norwegian.

The *Erling* with a whale tied to starboard. Image: William Spotswood Green

The huge body floated alongside the steamer's hull, the head lying agains her side,

The *Erling* and *Rusheen* with moored whales.
Image: Jack Leonard (1911), courtesy of Anthony Leonard

'Landing the whale' – still from *Whaling Afloat and Ashore*. Note the water spray on the right-hand side. The man on the right is moving any debris aside with a spade while another sprays water to avoid any damage to the body.

Robert Paul (1908), courtesy of the Irish Film Institute

Hamnavoe (or Handover)

Soft *airneál* pulls a reek of turf-ember from our clothes. Lobster pots, and us launching the currach onto *an bruth* as terns swerve and glide headlong to leeward. *Ar bord libh*, lads; sure, we could be rowing for America, and isn't drowning probable for any of us as the slit drift-nets washed up *ar an gcladach* after a squall, kelp-freighted, cool sea-rods plucked from the spray with their cure of iodine? *Crugaí* pivot with each plunge. We know them *bristeacha*, nightly boom that strafes our tarred ribs, *agus an cúr* into an eddying *tuaim*. Listen now for *an míol mór*; its slow plainsong, deepsea *caibleadh*, look for the bulge of its dive, wave-wallop *agus long báite, agus na Lochlannaigh, ar bord a gcuid galtáin*. Now, they're back again, the whale boatmen on the home stretch, slow lurch of surf gusting as the steamer pivots for Rusheen.

> Wind-time, tide-time, all Atlantean roars
> whale-time, work-time where a coal-boat is moored;
> our slaughter to their isle of grey and green.
> Morse code of rain; here, Rusheen.
> Dry-stone houses clammy with the plink
> of rain that weeps from ceiling to timber like a clock's tick.
>
> Skipper is the last ashore.
> Seán O'Donnell, ruler
> of the enisled roost, emerges.
> We unshackle the skrott, *hvalfanger*'s joy
> to the mooring buoy, and shake off
> the Atlantic on command.
> We're far from glacier and moraine
> and each inshore haven of our homeland.
> The islanders aren't glad for us
> but they are for the work,
> grunting a language that collides
> with ours as the swells break the shore.

Féach anois, us sinewy island lads, heave *an míol mór* up the slip, keep it wet so's not to tear the flimsy skin. We've pulled a calf this way: rope the limbs, work him out gentle so's not to wreck the animal. We need a forceful ease to land the *créatúr* into this world from its salty flood. Tobacco-tang sops to peat in our mouths as we move to a slurred rhythm of shiftwork. We swarm the lopsided bulk, scramble up the soaked knoll of its belly working as if the beast was merely asleep and we were to light fires on its deciduous back, still-fresh ribs frying savoury crackle on white sand. Superstition could claim this to be the case, that its barren back is a sea-girt oasis of mossy shade, a rudderless menagerie calved from Paradise.

Flense-time, furnace-time, a saint's voice drowned
by spume-spray, breaker-brawl, harpoon-bite
all under a cross-slab in its nook of weathered light,
oil-time, rib-time, another leviathan's dying sound.

Fins like flopped sails on blood-tinged sand, greyish and slimy to touch, its eyes jellied. The latter day Vikings peel the blanket of blubber back in strips. We lop it up to dripping chunks, juices hot as paraffin. Cut off meat and bone to boil. Jaw cracked. Feathery whalebone piled for scrubbing. Entrails unwound for burial and offal for *na muca*. Hear that coal bunker jangle as we wade through trenches of blood. At lunch, we dine among the dead, inhale the rot of giants, scoff sandwiches, swill bottled tae kept hot in a sock, and smoke as rain falls, silvery-smooth as a sliver of bait. The finback lies like a skerry, its slit belly agape as a cave.

Boilers fume with blubber, bone-time,
blade-time, sweaty legerdemain,
quitting-time, drinking-time,
scald of poitín in place of akvavit.

Export-time, profit-time, race against time
as dusk gives way to unworkable hours,
stars like flecks of coral lost to the waves
uncharted as the uncaught whales' watery graves.

The quay wall's beard of rust and birdshite, gulls scrumming for blubber scraps, relics of nordcaper and sei shorn of all flesh, choking the air. Out in *an Fharraige Mhór*, a fresh burst of wind brews black and unforeseen, gasping from *an ciúnáil* to drench and pour, blind as the swell drags millennia by millennia, the downing of tools, the satchels packed and we would not return. Chain of skill linking fathers of drowned sons far back to sea-rod and *caoirleach*. The island demands extravagance, and the station shall shut down in time: *ná beidh a leithéidí arís ann.*

'Flinching or removing the blubber' – still from *Whaling Afloat and Ashore*. Robert Paul (1908), courtesy of the Irish Film Institute

'Norwegian and Irish whalers at play' – still from *Whaling Afloat and Ashore*. Robert Paul (1908), courtesy of the Irish Film Institute

At play

Tomás Bán recalls an interaction between the locals and the Norwegians:

> I heard my dad tell me about two of the Inishkea men were out in the currach one day. Now, what they were doing was, they were transporting poitín. And the next thing, the Norwegians were passing in one of their whalers, you see, and they beckoned them over. And there was a big heave in the sea, like. So the two boys sailed over alongside anyway. They used to trade with them an odd time, like, you know. And sometimes when they wouldn't have time to fish themselves the Norwegian would buy the fish off them or they might buy lobster off them.
>
> The two boys came alongside anyway, and said the currach was going up and down and your man was gesturing above. They didn't know what he wanted, but he kept pointing. They must have seen them with the poitín. It was the poitín they were after. But when they done the exchange anyway, I remember Dad saying, he turned to the Norwegian and the Norwegian was going a mile a minute like, you know, and gesturing and he was happy and he said 'Aren't you the great speaker? But if there's a divil in hell, there's only one thing is that I don't know what it is you're saying.' One didn't know what the other was saying, but they knew enough.

Butchering Shanty
(Air: Preab san Ól)

O be it known
Ours was no Spitsbergen,
Norwegians held suspicion
Of our daily talk.
The station was abuzz
With all our purpose
As we dragged a carcass
Upon the bank.

Down on the slipway
Where the great beast lay
We stared down the day,
With blades a'ready.
Salt scrubbed our skin
As we got stuck in
With a nod and a grin
Our butcher's hand steady.

The titan lay prone
Its blubber like stone
We carved meat from bone
With a swing o' the blade.
Every slice and cut
Sent to the boiler's hut
Nearly burnt to soot
And all before the next raid.

Bone n' blubber, all 'cept stomach,
Barrelled gold the shade of muck
Boiled three times, as if for luck.
Our daily din the steel's slow swing.
We dry and scrub the jaw of baleen
Sacked to cinch the bellies of cailíns.
Bloody residue trickles back to sea
And we made a living from their dying.
As the day wore on

Under a sinking sun
We were far from done
With work unspoiled.
Oaths were muttered
As furnaces sputtered,
All the station cluttered
With blood and oil.

From the giant's bowels,
A treasure we'd unfold
Worth its weight in gold
O sweet ambergris!
And as for the guano
All our faces aglow
As we'd scoop and shovel
It out with ease.

Such latter-day Vikings,
Never done striving,
Harpoon guns kniving
Through the hunting ground
And through labour sifting,
Greased smoke drifting,
All our spirits lifting,
It's to the sea life we are bound.

The most enormous pigs

Opponents of the whaling stations objected on the grounds of pollution and a negative effect on the fishing. The hygiene issue was observed by the painter Paul Henry when he visited the island:

> This was appalling and so bad was it that it was a couple of months before I got it out of my clothes. There was a tremendous amount of offal which was being thrown to the pigs of which there were great numbers on the island, the most enormous pigs I ever saw. They were all over the shore dragging at the huge lumps of flesh with grunts and cries, and I was warned not to go near them they were so savage.[19]

Flensing [plan] & Inishkea whaling station Blacksod Belmullet Mayo.
Image: Jack Leonard, courtesy of Anthony Leonard

Flensing plan on Inishkea.
Image: William Spotswood Green

While the poor hygiene is evident, the fishing was only positively affected. In 1909, the lobster fishing was the best it had been in years. This may have affected the islanders decision to go on strike in August of that year, at the height of the season. As Tomás Bán puts it:

> If there was any hassle the Inishkea lads just downed tools and walked off, you know, take their currachs and a few pots and our way of fishing, you know, or something else. And if there was a wake on the island, sure, then they'd go for three days and they'd be pissed out of their minds when they come back! And you see, The Norwegians just couldn't understand this in fairness to them, like, you know. They were used to paying a weekly wage and a good wage it was. 15 shillings at that time was a great wage. They reckon the rent for the year that time was only a fiver, so it was mighty money for them.

Why, when two men on a currach could make £20 a week, would they choose butchering a whale carcass for 75p a week?

Edward Holt's inspection of the island during the strike found ten whales moored to the buoy, three to the pier, and one at the bottom of the slip, with a further two on the flensing plan. Wages were raised to £1 a week, but the result was short-lived.

SEPT 1911

Whales anchored in Bay at Inniskea Island
Blacksod ...

Whales anchored in Bay at Inniskea Island, Blacksod, Mayo.
Image: Jack Leonard, courtesy of Anthony Leonard

looked like a much smaller island, but proved
to be a number of dead whales moored ready

'Turning over the whale' – still from *Whaling Afloat and Ashore*. The body is being turned using chains to pull its massive weight. Two other partially flensed whales can be seen beside it.

Robert Paul (1908), courtesy of the Irish Film Institute

Sons of the Silent Shore

(Air: Eoghan Cóir)

Sing the song they never sang of us, boys, sing it unto the waves
Of Rusheen's misty strand, and of the men who hunted whales
O sing of the Irish hands, boys, who weathered through day and night
The sea's bounty to harvest as our boiler flames burned bright

> *Here's to the sons of the silent shore*
> *Who work through mist, wind and rain,*
> *Wild squalls howl, the sea spits its fury*
> *Bound to the whales by blade and chain*

'Twas the height of hunting season when the ships came ashore
Hauling finner carcasses up from the Atlantic's cold core
And by the flensing plan we stood in wait, a hardy crew
Our crowbars to hand, bloody work to pursue

> *Here's to the sons of the silent shore*
> *Who work through mist, wind and rain,*
> *Wild squalls howl, the sea spits its fury*
> *Bound to the whales by blade and chain*

With sinew and sweat, we laid tracks for the whales' hide
Winches hauled the beast up the slipway at low tide
Try pots bubbled liquid gold, oil brimming, precious gore
And from northern waters, blubber met the boiler's roar

> *Here's to the sons of the silent shore*
> *Who work through mist, wind and rain,*
> *Wild squalls howl, the sea spits its fury*
> *Bound to the whales by blade and chain*

All along Mayo's wild coast, the fire blazed like a beacon
From Fód Dubh to Inis Cé, mills rang with the crunch of bone
With rope-taut arms, we worked 'til our skin was whipped raw
To honour the beasts with our knives and the sea's cold law

Here's to the sons of the silent shore
Who work through mist, wind and rain,
Wild squalls howl, the sea spits its fury
Bound to the whales by blade and chain

So wetten your throats, boys, and rinse the song clean:
Raise your voices to the rough heroes of Rusheen
May our legacy endure, like waves that kiss this lonely strand
Where little remains of the toll on our land

WHA[...]

COAST OF IRELAND.

A NORWEGIAN REVIVAL OF A[...] IRISH
INDUSTRY SUBSIDISED BY
IRISH PARLIAMENT.   intelligent Islander.

these poor islands

Irishmen	cleanly view of life	weather,
Norwegians	deeply religious	good water,
	kindly race,	fine factory site,

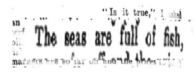

God bless the Norwegians; they have come,
and may they stay long."   industrious labour

Safe anchorage,

The blessing the fishery has been to these poor islands cannot be overestimated.

"Is it true," I asked

The seas are full of fish,

markets are so far off and the prices [...]

Text reads: 'Norwegian whaling off Iniskea Islands (N & S), visited by my father & myself from Dugort on 21/8/1912 JB.'
Joseph Brennan Album B, 1900. Courtesy of the National Library of Ireland

The seas are full of fish

Arranmore Whaling Company was not a success. In its most successful year, 1909, a loss of £2,042 was recorded. The consensus seems to be that the islanders themselves posed a difficulty. While the islanders' reluctance to cooperate can't have helped, there were other difficulties with the station. Rusheen was tidal, and the hours it could be worked on were limited for this reason. There was also a lack of fresh water. To resolve this issue, two concrete dams were built across streams on Inishkea South, and remain there to this day.

The station was poorly managed, with blood running into the sea and blubber fragments cast around the beach. While some improvements were made, problems remained. A profit was turned in 1911, but in 1912 only 26 whales were caught. The company dissolved and reformed under the same name twice.

In 1913, a catch of just 49 whales spelled the end. Nolan notes that 'the islanders were accused of helping themselves liberally to the moveables – even the corrugated iron from the roofs.'[20]

Tomás reflects:

> I don't think the Inishkeas were sad to see them going, you know. But, of course, nobody turns down employment. Especially in them days, in hard times. There was no dole that time or when the pension came in 1908 started and you didn't get that until you were 70 years of age.

The islanders would return to their way of life, fishing and trading poitín, until 1927 when a storm claimed the lives of ten of their men, leading to the eventual evacuation of the islands.

Blacksod Whaling Company

A serious and unnecessary risk

Mayo Whaling Stations.

THE NORWEGIAN NUISANCE

———

A DOUBLE DANGER.

OUTBREAK OF PLAGUE.

———

FISHERIES RUINED.

———

ACTION OF MAYO COUNTY COUNCIL

a menace to the public health

ruinous to the fishing

will bring a plague

dangerous stuff   livelihood

prohibited.

intolerable.

will ruin

is calculated to make

life in the district

the lives of the people[21]

The man behind Blacksod Whaling Company was Lorentz Bruun, an experienced seaman who had been the skipper on one of the Inishkea whalers. He was charming, a hunter, and counted the wealthy Glasgow businessmen Leslie Hamilton Wilson among his business associates. He purchased land at Ardelly point on the mainland from landlord Denis (Dinny) Bingham. Bingham wasn't well off for his class, and the finances were welcome.

a serious and unnecessary risk

the whaling company
endangers the health
of the people

forcing stations on the Irish
not
allowed
anywhere on the English coast.

Objections rolled in quickly. The Collooney-Blacksod Railway Company, Mayo County Council, and two of Bingham's neighbours were at the forefront. Claims were made that the smell of the Inishkea station reached the mainland, and that entrails of whales washed up all along the coast of the mullet. Henry Richards expressed concern over the fisheries and contamination of the coast.

Since evidence from Inishkea showed that the fishing had only improved, objections from fisheries soon receded, and the support from the community was unfailing as it was the first prospect of steady employment in the area.

Lorentz Bruun and his highly skilled lawyer soon dealt with the objectors and a licence was granted in August 1909. Whaling started in 1910.

Very nice men

Blacksod Whaling Station. Structures from right to left: slipway, boilerhouse, oil store, guano dryer, fire-house, men's quarters.
Image courtesy of Patrick Geraghty

The station at Elly was more efficiently run than its island counterpart, at least in the beginning. Bruun was an experienced businessman, and being on the mainland the poor hygiene that occurred at Inishkea would not have made the station many friends.

There were 30 Norwegians and 15-20 Irishmen working at the station. The rate of pay was 15 shillings, as on Inishkea before the strike, though this varied depending on the skill of the job. Flensers received the most. More men were needed at the beginning as the station was constructed. With the exception of the concrete flensing plan and the brick ovens and chimneys, everything was made of wood. The Norwegians were blacksmiths, carpenters, engineers, and even a baker. They brought all their own food, beans, potatoes, flour, and coffee. The baker made bread and pastries. Meat was purchased locally and whale meat was also consumed.

A worker of the station, William Meenaghan, worked hours 4.15am to 8pm. He said the men would eat at 5.30am, 8am, 12pm, 3pm, and 6.30pm. Three meals and two breaks of coffee and a roll. They worked roughly 60 hours a week.[22]

The Norwegians and Irish mingled more than at the Inishkea station. Another worker, James Monaghan recalled, 'The Norwegians are great seamen, and very nice men, but some of them, on Sunday, used to take good bit of drink, you know, and they would dress very well on Sunday.'[23]

Mr Barrett lived up the road from the station. He was a cooper on the station in 1920 and 1922. He said that the Norwegians were nice men who he would drink with once a week in a pub owned by an ex-RIC man.

Ted Sweeney, who was a schoolboy in the area at the time, remembered how 'the Norwegians occasionally used to come up to Blacksod for a weekend and have a hooley.'[24]

A shocking beast

SS *Erris.* Image: Leslie Hamilton Wilson (1911), courtesy of the Johnson Museum

The harpoon was supposed to weigh 80lbs and had three or four barbs that could open up at the end. There was explosive at the tip, which exploded in the whale. After they came out of the whale, they were often bent, and some whales arrived with as many as three harpoons in them. However, the additional harpoons were ones which had not hit the right spot, and had had to be cut loose. The harpoons were nearly always bent and had to be straightened at the forge they had at the station.[25]

– *Notes of Dr James Fairley interview with Mr Meenaghan and Martin Broderick, 1978*

Loading the harpoon gun.
Image: Leslie Hamilton Wilson (1911), courtesy of the Johnson Museum

Smoke from the gun.
Image: Leslie Hamilton Wilson (1911), courtesy of the Johnson Museum

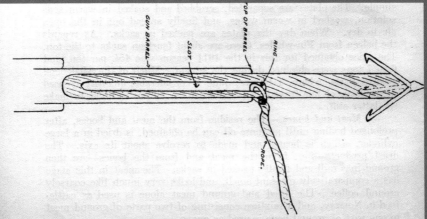

FIG. 3.—Harpoon (in gun) (approx. $\frac{1}{11}$ nat. size).

three movable hooked barbs, and an arrangement by which an explosive shell is attached, the shell exploding inside the body of the whale.

The harpoon is attached to a strong 3-inch hempen rope, which is run round a winch on deck and then over a pulley arrangement attached to the foremast, the further end of the rope being fastened to a long, strong spring fixed along the bottom of the boat. This latter is to prevent any great amount of jarring when the rope is run out.

The fin-whales, when dead, generally sink, except they be very fat. They are hauled up from the bottom, a pipe is thrust into the body cavity, and air is pumped in, the hole being afterwards plugged. The whales are towed tail foremost, generally alongside the boat, but in rough weather they are towed astern. The tail-flukes are cut off immediately on capture, to lessen the resistance to towing.

The harpoons are not fired at a longer range than about 50 yards, so that great skill is required in manœuvring the ship. An attempt is made to shoot just as the whale begins to dive downwards, and to hit, if possible, just behind the shoulder.

S.T. Burfield (1912)

The ships would go to sea and stay out until they either had enough whales to tow back to shore or were running low on coal. They were usually away for three or four days. Reportedly, a boat was once gone a whole week. There wasn't wireless onboard, and its fate was unknown. It eventually returned, with a whale, having had to take shelter from a storm on an island to the north.[26]

The crew on the whalers consisted of eight Norwegians. A man kept watch in the crows nest and shouted when he saw a whale. The captain was the only one to use the harpoon.

Ideally, the explosive tip of the harpoon would kill the whale quickly. If a whale was shot and not killed, it would swim ahead, so it was important that the boat follow at full speed. A man had the job of standing in the bow with a hatchet, prepared to cut the harpoon cable in the scenario that the tethered whale sounded and pulled the boat below. If the rope began to grow slack, they would know the whale was dead and could be winched in.

The dead whale was inflated and attached by a chain around the tail to the side of the ship. If there was more whaling to do, they might leave the carcass tethered to a buoy and collect it on the return journey. The ships would bring two or more whales back to the station, one on each side of the ship and more being towed behind. They would unload their cargo, refill their bunkers with coal, and go back to sea.

Whalers were fast ships. They cut a channel in the water when going at full speed. Cargo ships brought coal, unloaded into a hulk anchored in the bay, before refilling with barrels of oil and bags of manure and bringing them away to Scotland.

Opposite: A 70-foot fin whale.
Image: Leslie Hamilton Wilson (1911), courtesy of the Johnson Museum

The first cut. Image: Leslie Hamilton Wilson (1911), courtesy of the Johnson Museum

When a whale was killed, it was towed back to the station and buoyed in the bay until the factory workers were ready for it. Every part of the whale was utilised. The whales were winched onto the plane while being sprayed with water to avoid damage to the thin skin. Norwegians and some Irish men flensed the animal, separating the strips of blubber from the carcass with specialised knives. The strips were pulled away by winch before being cut into manageable chunks and transported up the elevator to the boilers.

In the first seasons, the Norwegians did the specialised work of flensing, but they taught the work to the locals, and fewer Norwegians did the work as time went on.

The whales were turned using crowbars that stood as tall as a man. Tanks were placed below the flensing plan to collect the runoff. One man had the job of collecting this liquid, boiling it, and siphoning off the oil. In the 1911 season, the sale of this oil alone was worth £600. The meat was separated from the blubber. The meat-flenser then removed the head, and the meat from the bones. The meat and bones were chopped, boiled and ground down to make guano, a substance used as cattle feed or fertiliser. When the meat was fresh it could be, and was, eaten at the station. The Norwegians would take cuts of meat and salt them to bring home at the end of the season. The baleen was cleaned and dried and sold to France. It was a low-price commodity and processing the baleen was done on slow days. In 1914, a 15lb mass of ambergris was found in one of the sperm whales landed. Sperm whales were the most valuable catch, largely because of the spermaceti in their heads.

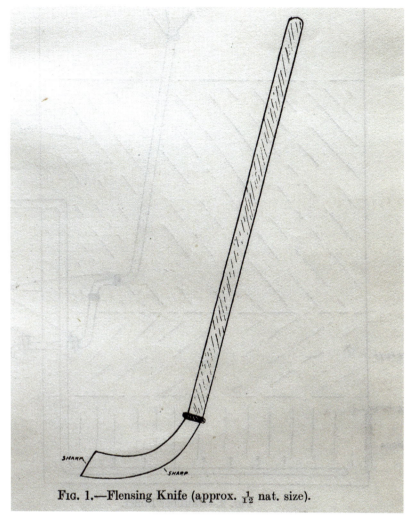

FIG. 1.—Flensing Knife (approx. $\frac{1}{12}$ nat. size).

S.T. Burfield (1912)

Mr Meenaghan described the removal of spermaceti from the carcass. 'There used to be many barrels of oil taken from the head of a sperm whale. A 'trough' was placed against the sperm whale's head, and this led into a concrete tank which was kept heated – the tank, not the head. The oil would run out fairly fast for a day or so, then a man would cut the head open further with a knife and the oil would start to flow again.'[27]

The bones of sperm whales were used to make walking sticks. According to Ted Sweeney, they were polished 'with fancy tops with heads and ships carved on the handles. The craft came in with the Norwegians but some of the locals were very quick to take it up.'[28]

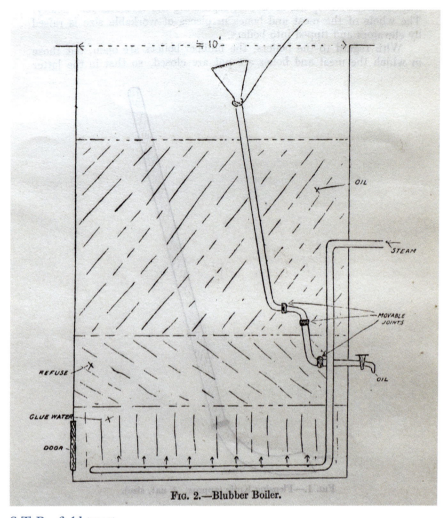

FIG. 2.—Blubber Boiler.

S.T. Burfield (1912)

1910

Elly Bay Whaling station Belmullet mayo

Elly Bay whaling station, Belmullet Mayo. Fin whale on the flensing plan, note the blanket of blubber being removed. Behind it is the boiler house, with two elevators to bring the blubber and meat to the boilers.
Image: Jack Leonard, courtesy of Anthony Leonard

'The whale is a shocking beast and many people came from near and far to see them at the station, from as far as Ballina and Dublin. On Saturday evening, supposing a whale was at anchor out in the tide, they would bring it up for people to look at on Sunday.

'The jetty was built with wood and stones were packed underneath. They had a slip to bring up the whale. This was made of concrete. There were two winches to pull up the whales. The place where the whale was brought was smooth and level. The station and boilers were alongside this. Standing alongside the whale, you would barely see the top of the chimney.'[29]

Carcase [carcass] consisting of the entrails.

Image: Leslie Hamilton Wilson (1911), courtesy of the Johnson Museum

Some of the chief opposers, including Henry Richards and Father McHale, became supporters of the company. Richards benefitted from the digging up of entrails to use as fertiliser.

Inspectors of the Fisheries Branch surveyed the marine flora and fauna between 1909 and 1911 to monitor pollutants from the factory. The only changes were found within 200 yards of the shore and were minimal. The station also worked with biologists, and their reports continue to provide scientists with valuable information about cetaceans.

Capture No.	Date	Length of Adult		Length of Fœtus		Sex of Fœtus
		Ft.	in.	Ft.	in.	
14	July 12	70	9	8	11	♂
16	July 16	74	9	4	11	♀
18	July 20	65	7	8	5	♀
25	July 24	66	8	6	0	♀
33	Aug. 7	75	0	5	6	?
37	Aug. 11	66	0	9	0	♀
49	Sept. 10	68	9	9	0	♀
51	Sept. 18	67	8	9	3	♂

TABLE XI.—*Balœnoptera musculus* (L.). Fœtuses.

S.T. Burfield (1912)

Whale on the dock.
Image: Leslie Hamilton Wilson (1911), courtesy of the Johnson Museum

'A female with unborn young gives the best yield [of oil], whilst a female with a suckling probably yields the least.'[30]

Workers at Elly Bay Whaling Station, Co. Mayo.
Image from house of Patrick Geraghty

Local man Patrick Geraghty at home, holding a crowbar from Blacksod Station. Implement used for turning the whale carcasses. Pictured 2024

Workers at Elly Bay Whaling Station, Co. Mayo.
Image courtesy of Patrick Geraghty

(Gel)ousy burned it down

Despite the improvements on the Arranmore Co. station, it was not immune to politics, both local and global. In 1914, 89 whales were caught, but war broke out in Europe and it was ordered that all British fishing vessels must have British crew. This was, of course, before Irish independence. There was no more whaling until after the war.

When whaling recommenced, production costs had gone up and the price of oil had slumped. Repairs needed to be done to the station, which had been used as a petrol base during the war, and no whaling happened in 1919. Bruun was no longer actively engaged in the running of the station, having business elsewhere. In 1920, their best year, they caught 125 whales and produced 3995 barrels of oil. The company still registered a loss.

However, in 1920 the station employed 100 locals, three times as many as before the war. According to former worker Mr Monaghan, the 'people of the land' put pressure on the Norwegians to employ more men than were needed. The Norwegians had 'no say at all.'[31]

While the world at large was at war, there was plenty of conflict on a smaller scale here in Ireland. Local man Pap Murphy of the Turas Siar heritage centre recalls the complexities of the community at the time:

> There were two factions in the area and there was conflict because of that. They'd been out shooting each other down the bog.

This was the time of the Irish War of Independence. Pap tells us that there had been conflict around the station due to the inevitably limited number of jobs. There was competition for the work as there was so little employment available in the area. He refers to people being ambushed and assaulted so they were unable to work, and their job may go to someone else.

> Money was always the reason. Especially out here on the coast.

In an impoverished part of a country still extracting itself from colonialism, a man's political background informed whether or not he got work.

Dennis Bingham, the local landlord, was also the paymaster at the station. Monaghan said he had a 'big say in things.' The workers of the time spoke well of Bingham, but he was a part of the landed gentry, a class that was on the decline. Alice Bruun recalled the Binghams having trouble during the war of independence. William Meenaghan said there had been a 'threat to Bingham by IRA or similar people; apparently it was a demand for Bingham's guns.'[32]

In February 1923, a large part of the station was burned down. Father Dodd, the parish priest, condemned the act from the pulpit. He's said to have claimed that whoever caused the fire 'won't carry a candle to the grave.'[33]

In *Within the Mullet*, Rita Nolan says, 'Local people said jealousy burned it down. Bingham, whose loss was greater than most, was not impressed. His hay rick had been burned down a short time before, reputedly by the same arsonists. Not a word of condemnation had been uttered by the priest. Denis Bingham said, "If he spoke then the station would still be there, employing 100 people".'[34]

It is difficult not to make a link between the burning and the *Freeman's Journal* article in 1909, which quotes the chairman of Mayo County Council saying that Norwegian stations had been burned down and that men had 'a sacred right to protect their industry and families if threatened by danger from any quarter.'[35]

It is tempting to interpret cause or prophecy, but 14 years had passed during which the station had provided employment and caused little disruption. The opposition had largely dissolved. Tomás Bán points out that the fire must be taken in the context of the time:

> That was 1923. They also burned Bingham's Castle. I'd say they had a bit of petrol left over and went and burned the station! That was when the land wars were starting and there was agitation with land and all that. That was after the Free State had been formed. There was a lot of hassle on the Mullet to get the grazers out. The Irish league and all that.

In Dr Fairley's interview with former workers Mr Meenaghan and Mr Broderick, he notes, 'The station is supposed to have been burned down by three men living close to, and to the east of, Tíraun church. They were refused jobs in the whaling station, and burned it down out of spite. All three were drowned in the bay together, later.'[36]

Pap gives us yet another insight into the story. 'Three men were drowned at sea and the finger was pointed at them.'

But it was not after their accusation that they drowned, but the other way around. These three men had all been employed at the station. This contradicts the idea that it was jealousy from men who had been refused employment that caused the fire.

The cause of the fire was not proven, and much of the facts have been lost with time. As Pap says, the real story may never come out. However, 'the major part of the Elly Bay station was burned, according to local report, accidentally whilst a number of men were searching for explosives believed to be in the factory.'[37]

'Gelignite,' Pap says, nodding. The explosives used in the head of the harpoon could prove quite useful during a war. A tragic irony must be noted here, as one of the primary sources of gelignite at the time was, in fact, whale oil.

The company was losing money, and as with other whaling stations, the water was running out of whales. With the loss of the station, it seemed inevitable that whaling off the coast of Mayo must come to an end. The Norwegians returned home or set off on ventures further south. The Mayo families were once again without reliable employment. The whales were left be from this particular threat.

MACHINERY.[38]

DISMANTLING Elly Bay Whaling Station, Blacksod, Co. Mayo.—Steel, Timber and Galvanised Buildings. Steam Engines and Boilers: 11 Digesters: numerous Steel Pans and Tanks fitted with Heating Coils: Steel Drying Cylinder about 40 feet long by 6 feet diameter; Elevators and Blowers. Very large quantity of Timber, Galvanised Sheets, etc. For further particulars apply—Thos. W. Ward, Ltd., 45/46 City Quay, Dublin. Telephone No. 43878: or our Foreman on the Job.

Watcher as amateur archaeologist

We drive down multiple small laneways, make awkward three-point turns that nearly spill us into the ditch. I stop, one eye flicking to the rearview mirror, and check Google maps again. I switch the format to the satellite shot so I might get a more accurate image of where we're going, but it's just green squares, more heavily pixelated than most videogames.

Another road turns to overgrown track and ends with a gate to a field.

'Here?' I say to Mariner. He nods and I tuck the car as far off the road as I can.

There's no clear path to the water. A woman comes out of her cottage.

We explain. She nods. Tells us to go through her field, but warns we won't find anything there but stones.

The fields drop to the beach. Machair cut with concrete, and bricks, or their remains, rounded to bulbous sea pebbles, coronation red, split and rolled by water. Broken down, in a gathering of grit, the water rusted to blood.

I scan the scene for sense.

A hint that we are near the moored meat, the flensing plan, the shifting talus of time.

Smoke curls from a lone cigarette. Flakes of boilers oxidise in the brine.

Oil and water

If the station hadn't met its end in the manner it did, I wonder if it would have continued. Would whaling in Ireland still exist today? Or would they simply have run out of whales? Norway's economy was to drastically change by the middle of the century when their own oil reserves were discovered.

It's difficult not to see the parallels between whaling and the fossil fuel industry. Exploitation of a resource, companies operating at large scale in countries that don't have the finances to benefit from the industry themselves. The push for profit in the face of adverse effects. And, of course, oil. Energy. The apparent point of it all.

Were the whales saved by the thing that is now, almost two centuries later, bringing life on earth towards mass extinction?

In Burfield's report at the Blacksod station, there is an account on the opinion on extinction of the whales at the time. 'In view of the large numbers of the largest kinds of Cetacea which are now killed every year, the question of their probable extinction in the course of comparatively few years must be seriously considered. With a view to preventing this possible extinction there is some discussion as to legislation in Norway and England. …Naturally, the proposed limitation of the whale-hunting does not meet with the approval of the whalers. According to them the whaling in the Northern stations will cease automatically before the extinction takes place… The underlying idea seems to be that of a definite number of whales passing over a given area at one time, only a certain percentage ever caught, on account of the difficulty in locating the animals and the chances of the chase. As the total number of animals passes over a given area becomes fewer, the percentage actually caught will fall. The conclusion drawn is that this fall will cause the minimum catch per boat to be reached before the total extinction takes place. How far this reasoning is sound is doubtful, but I give it as it was given to me.'[39]

Whaling did not stop with the discovery of crude oil. More whales were killed in the 20th century than in all previous centuries of industrialised whaling. Commercial whaling reached its peak in the 1960s, a century after the discovery of oil. Three million whales were killed in the 20th century.

Fossil fuels, contrary to popular belief, were not replacing whale oil. While petroleum began to replace whale oil as a light source, there were other uses for the whales, and the fossil fuel-powered technologies made it easier and faster to kill them.

The basic principles of capitalism rest on supply and demand. If your supply surpasses demand, you're at a bust. Unless, that is, demand changes. In 'Why Petroleum Did Not Save the Whales', Richard York notes that 'Perhaps one of the most widely recognized features of the modern era is the ability of private industry to innovate and develop new consumer goods and markets. So, it should not be surprising that despite the rise of fossil fuels, new uses were regularly found for the raw materials provided by whalers.'[40]

The ever-increasing technologies available brought the opportunity for more oil to be used. There was room in the market for both whale and fossil. Hydrogenation allowed for whale oil to be used in the manufacturing of margarine and soap. Another opportunity for the whaling industry struck with war. Glycerine is a byproduct of soap manufacturing. It is also used to make explosives. Whales were being killed so people could kill each other.

While earning money was undoubtedly a leading cause in the exploitation of the whales, there were geopolitical aspects to the industry. York likens it to the tragedy of the commons. The industry was unregulated. The whales migrated across the boundaries countries had created to declare ownership of the ocean.

As York explains, 'Whales were overexploited because individual nations and whalers benefited from killing whales but did not reap the long-term rewards of conservation if they practiced restraint, since others continued whaling regardless.'[41]

The Soviet whaling of the 20th century was motivated by politics more than profit. Stalin's mass industrialisation meant production targets were set that related more to the amount of whales caught than the usable product. There was a nationalist urge to get their share of whales, killing them not for profit, but so that other countries could not profit from them.

The competition and sheer scale of whaling after the Second World War decimated the global populations. It was clear that whaling was near the end as there just weren't enough whales. This caused individual whaling nations to hunt even more, to maximise profit before the opportunity was lost. The International Convention for the Regulation of Whaling was created in 1946 to 'provide for the proper conservation of whale stocks and thus make possible the orderly development of the whaling industry.'[42]

The International Whaling Commission was formed in 1949. When a moratorium was finally put in place, in 1982, whales were commercially extinct. The whaling industry was all but done, and conservation was a small commitment from most of the nations who agreed to it.

Yet not all countries joined the IWC. Whaling is still a way of asserting political power. Why would Norway, Iceland, Japan, or Russia listen to the US on whaling, when the US no longer has a whaling industry?

Whaling can't be thought of as a singular entity based on need any more than the fossil fuel industry. It's in the interest of those who profit from fossil fuels to believe that whaling declined due to available alternatives. It is a widely held belief that green energy will naturally suppress oil and gas. Even, as York notes, 'former president Barack Obama (2017) argues that clean energy will inevitably push fossil fuels out of the market.'[43]

Yet empirical evidence suggests otherwise. While clean energy sources are discovered and developed, fossil fuel extraction is still increasing.

Looking at Burfield's report we can see that the idea that the market will sort itself out naturally is not a new belief. Perhaps whaling would have come to a stop when it was no longer profitable, but the assumption that this would happen before the species were extinct was incorrect.

Would the whalers have persisted until the last whale was dead? Will the fossil fuel industry withdraw every litre of oil, of gas, unless prevented?

OF
STORM
AND
WATER

Sanctuary

The word has such religious connotations, it's all I can think of when I hear it. Some divine rest from persecution. Sanctuary differs from home or habitat because of that definition. It is a place of safety when elsewhere is unsafe. It is a place of refuge when you are under attack.

The concept of a cetacean sanctuary originated in the early 20th century. Like other restrictions on whaling, it was proposed to preserve whaling stocks.

'Sr. Jose Leon Suarez, an eminent Argentine lawyer, was its pathfinder in the 1920s. He was the reporter of a commission to the League on whether it is possible to establish by way of international agreement rules regarding the exploitation of the products of the sea'. Sr. Suarez wanted to create a "new jurisprudence", and in doing so made an impassioned and historic plea for conservation.

'He suggested that in addition to bringing whaling under international control, a sanctuary for whales should be declared in the Antarctic.'[44]

The original sanctuary was reopened to whalers in 1955 due to pressure from whaling nations who had cleared stocks in the other oceans. It was a safe haven no more. It wasn't until a 'surge of global environmental consciousness in the early 1970s' that the concept was revisited in practice.

IRELAND - EUROPE'S FIRST WHALE SANCTUARY

Only three months after the Irish Whale and Dolphin Group proposal, An Taoiseach, Charles Haughey declared Irish territorial waters a whale and dolphin sanctuary. This is an unprecedented step within Europe and has many important implications for the global conservation of whales and dolphins. The first official whale sanctuary was declared in 1913 in Western Australia as a method of conserving stocks for commercial exploitation. Since the successful establishment of the Indian Ocean Whale sanctuary in 1979, sanctuary areas have been declared off the coasts of Mexico, U.S.A., Ecuador, Dominican Republic and Canada. However the Irish declaration has set a precedence as it incorporates the state's entire exclusive fishery zone. We will have to wait and see if other maritime nations will follow Ireland's example. Here is the full text of the sanctuary declaration from the Department of the Taoiseach, dated 7th June, 1991:

The Taoiseach announced today that the Government have declared all our seas a Whale and Dolphin Sanctuary. This Declaration is in conformity with the Government's Environmental Action Plan Programme and the Dublin Declaration on the Environment which was adopted by the European Council during Ireland's Presidency of the European Community in June, 1990. It is a clear indication of Ireland's commitment to contribute to the preservation and protection of these magnificent creatures in their natural environment, and to do everything possible to ensure that they should not be put in danger of extinction but should be preserved for future generations. Ireland already has a comprehensive legal framework in place - the Whale Fisheries Act, 1937, and the Wildlife Act, 1976 - which empowers the Government to provide this sanctuary. Under this legislation, the hunting of all whale species, including dolphins and porpoises, has been totally banned within the exclusive fishery limits of the State i.e. out to 200 miles from the coast. The Declaration of the Whale and Dolphin Sanctuary within the exclusive fishery limits of the entire country is the first in Europe and will, hopefully, be followed by other maritime nations. The Taoiseach congratulated the recently - established Irish Whale and Dolphin Group for their role in promoting the study and conservation of whales and dolphins in Irish coastal waters.

At the recent meeting of the International Whaling Commission in Iceland, Ireland took the position that the moratorium on commercial whaling in international waters, begun in 1986, should continue. Some 10 years ago

Ireland joined The International Whaling Commission, the aim of which is to provide for the proper conservation of whales throughout the world and for the orderly development of the whaling industry in that context. Ireland's efforts on both the national and international fronts, therefore, have ensured that we are making a significant contribution to the world wide conservation of whales and dolphins.

Reactions to the Whale Sanctuary declaration

"We are now waking up to the richness of the warm-blooded life around our shores"
- Michael Viney.
"It is a very welcome move to protect the whales and dolphins, but the Irish fishing fleet also needs protection"
- Mary O'Donnell, Green Party
"While welcoming the principle of establishing such a sanctuary, failure to consult with representatives of the fishing industry was 'irresponsible' and 'high-handed' and can only be described as 'the thin end of the wedge'"
- Joey Murrin, chief executive, Killybegs Fishermen's Organisation.
"Did Fungi have something to do with it?"
- Tom MacSweeny, Marine Times.
"We need concrete enforcement measures to make sure the navy is given the directive to use the power it has and for it not to turn a blind eye to whaling activities"
- Jeremy Wates, Co-ordinator of Earthwatch.
"There is understandable anxiety about how such a sanctuary situation might conflict with commercial fishing operations which do not wish to harm these creatures"
- Editorial, Marine Times.

IRISH WHALE AND DOLPHIN GROUP

Newsletter, September 1991

Ireland – Europe's first whale sanctuary

Only three months after the Irish Whale and Dolphin Group proposal, An Taoiseach, Charles Haughey declared Irish territorial waters a whale and dolphin sanctuary. This is an unprecedented step within Europe and has many important implications for the global conservation of whales and dolphins. The first official whale sanctuary was declared in 1913 in Western Australia as a method of conserving stocks for commercial exploitation. Since the successful establishment of the Indian Ocean Whale sanctuary in 1979, sanctuary areas have been declared off the coasts of Mexico, U.S.A., Ecuador, Dominican Republic and Canada. However the Irish declaration has set a precedence as it incorporates the state's entire exclusive fishery zone. We will have to wait and see if other maritime nations will follow Ireland's example. Here is the full text of the sanctuary declaration from the Department of the Taoiseach, dated 7th June, 1991:

> The Taoiseach announced today that the Government have declared all our seas a Whale and Dolphin Sanctuary. This Declaration is in conformity with the Government's Environmental Action Plan Programme and the Dublin Declaration on the Environment which was adopted by the European Council during Ireland's Presidency of the European Community in June, 1990. It is a clear indication of Ireland's commitment to contribute to the preservation and protection of these magnificent creatures in their natural environment, and to do everything possible to ensure that they should not be put in danger of extinction but should be preserved for future generations. Ireland already has a comprehensive legal framework in place – the Whale Fisheries Act, 1937, and the Wildlife Act, 1976, - which empowers the Government to provide this sanctuary. Under this legislation, the hunting of all whale species, including dolphins and porpoises, has been totally banned within the exclusive fishery limits of the State i.e. out of 200 miles from the coast. The Declaration of the Whale and Dolphin Sanctuary within the exclusive fishery limits of the entire country is the first in Europe and will hopefully, be followed by other maritime nations. The Taoiseach congratulated the recently established Irish Whale and

Dolphin Group for their role in promoting the study and conservation of whales and dolphins in Irish coastal waters.

At the recent meeting of the International Whaling Commission in Iceland, Ireland took the position that the moratorium on commercial whaling in international waters, begun in 1986, should continue. Some 10 years ago Ireland joined The International Whaling Commission, the aim of which is to provide the proper conservation of whales throughout the world and for the orderly development of the whaling industry in that context. Ireland's efforts on both the national and international fronts, therefore, have ensured that we are making a significant contribution to the world wide conservation of whales and dolphins.

Reactions to the Whale Sanctuary declaration

"We are now waking up to the richness of the warm-blooded life around our shores."
– Michael Viney

"It is very welcome move to protect the whales and dolphins, but the Irish fishing fleet also needs protection."
– Mary O'Donnell, Green Party

"While welcoming the principle of establishing such a sanctuary, failure to consult with representatives of the fishing industry was 'irresponsible' and 'high-handed' and can only be described as 'the thin end of the wedge."
– Joey Murrin, chief executive, Killybegs Fisherman's Organisations

"Did Fungi have something to do with it?"
– Tom MacSweeny, *Marine Times*

"We need concrete enforcement measures to make sure the navy is given the directive to use the power it has and for it not to turn a blind eye to whaling activates."
– Jeremy Wates, co-ordinator of Earthwatch

"There is understandable anxiety about how such a sanctuary situation might conflict with commercial fishing operations which do not wish to harm these creatures."
– Editorial, *Marine Times*

Land and sea

Land is never owned, only claimed.

Environmentalists often come up against land ownership. Who is to tell the owner of a field that they can't cut their grass or spray fertiliser? Especially in a country with a history of occupation and displacement.

Growing up in the Mayo countryside, most houses around us were linked in one way or another to farming. While my mother taught me bird names, she cursed the boom of the hedge cutter shredding their nests.

The corncrake was pushed to the brink of extinction in Ireland due to industrial farming. I was aware of the threat to birds and insects because of pesticides, cut hedgerows, agricultural colonisation of the countryside. Native species such as pine martens were shot by farmers in case they killed their lambs. Gorse fires, though illegal, annually decimate vast swathes of countryside. No matter. When the government is voted in by those whose livelihood depends on agriculture, little is done.

In a country where the people once couldn't own their own land, land ownership means everything. Belonging. Survival. Power.

I was ten years old the first time I became aware of north Mayo being a sort of separate entity, its vastness and distinction one to rival west Cork. The county was abuzz with the Corrib gas controversy. Already anxious about pollution and environmental collapse, the proximity of the proposed gas line terrified me. I knew the very basics. A corporation, money for the powers that be, local people outraged and afraid. The people who lived on the land had no say. When the state ruled something for the greater good, what did ownership matter?

Seventy years after the whaling industry finished its work on the Mullet, the area again attracted the interest of foreign business. In 1996, The Corrib natural gas field was discovered by Enterprise Oil, 52 miles northwest of the Mullet peninsula. It would be the beginning of a controversy that would last decades.

Where whaling was once the commercial connection between Ireland and Norway, however briefly, a parallel now emerges with the Norwegian and Irish gas fields. When Norwegian reserves of North Sea oil were discovered in the 1960s, the state responded by creating its own oil company. This ensured that the country profited directly from the extraction. Norway is now not only one of the richest countries in the world, but its citizens are also said to enjoy one of the highest standards of living.

In 1975, Minister Justin Keating introduced Ireland's first oil and gas legislation. It was modelled on international best practice. It included a 50 percent tax rate and the right for the state to acquire 50 percent of the reserves. The profits of fossil fuels drilled at the site would, in theory, benefit the country as a whole. But the government changed, and the new Minister for Energy, Ray Burke, removed royalties on petroleum and gas extraction.

Ministers Ray Burke and Bertie Ahern changed Irish law in 1987 and 1992 so that multinational companies own 100 percent of the oil and gas they find under Irish waters. Companies can write off 100 percent of their costs against tax and have profits taxed at 25 percent compared to the international average of 68 percent. They can export oil and gas outside of Ireland and sell to Bord Gáis at full market rate. Burke admitted to private consultations with oil companies. It has been described as 'the great gas giveaway'. At the time, Burke's actions were described by Dick Spring as 'an act of economic treason'. Mr Burke was later jailed for corruption charges on an unrelated matter.

Local people weren't happy with a lack of clarity around the project. Untreated gas would be piped to a processing plant on land. This would run through private land, and a Special Conservation Area. Corrib Gas/Shell to Sea would be a 20-plus year controversy that has been well documented, but remains unsettled. Some of the key points of the controversy include:

- Compulsory acquisition by a private company – for the first time in the history of the state
- The Rossport Five, five men who refused Shell access to work on their land, were jailed at the request of Shell
- Allegations of abuses of power by An Garda Síochána

I'd been aware of the controversy, of the harrowing corruption of it all. I thought, as I always did, of the birds, the otters, the people. I didn't think of whales. They were the stuff of colder climates, exotic places. Even knowing they dwell in Irish waters, it is difficult to comprehend the struggles of something so otherworldly, so removed from the land beneath us. There were those who drew attention to the negative impacts of deep-sea drilling on animals who use sonar to communicate. Journalist Lorna Siggins reported on the matter at the time, and later included it in her book, *Once Upon a Time in the West.*

> The IWDG appealed to the government to apply the EU's Environmental Impact Assessment Directive to seismic surveys and exploration drilling in Ireland's marine territory. It called on the minister for arts, heritage, the Gaeltacht and the islands to stop further development of the onshore aspects of the Corrib gas terminal until a survey of cetaceans had been carried out.

> 'At present there is another seismic survey under way off north-west Mayo as part of the Corrib gas-field development, and there is no attempt to assess or mitigate this impact on cetaceans,' IWDG director Dr Simon Berrow told *The Irish Times* of 6 June 2001.

> 'We know the area is used by a wide range of cetacean species, including pilot and minke whales and white-sided, common and bottle-nosed dolphins, and that seismic activity may displace whales and dolphins from their preferred habitat.'[45]

The effect on cetaceans, no more than the effect on people, was not sufficient reason to halt the project.

I wonder now about the connection between the whaling station and the gas line. I'm aware of my poet's inclination to compare. Yet I suspect neither a whaling station nor an untreated gas line would touch the shores of South Dublin. North Mayo is isolated, which makes it an easy victim of abuse and neglect. Now I am a woman thinking of what happens when someone wants to abuse you, keep you isolated, your voice small and unheard.

Watcher as morbidity tourist

Sperm whale, Cross Beach, Co. Mayo, April 2023

It floats like driftwood across my laptop screen.
I gasp, grab my car keys, coat, boots.
Where bog-red stream collides with flood
current — sand to shallow to deep — he floats.
Like a baby rocked to amniotic laps. A lazy flick
of tail, trick of the eye, gust of water. White, pink,
the lichenous stain of country cottages. Grey skin
shaken off like a winter coat, now he's a regular Moby Dick.
This is the first time I've been close. And still, I can't touch.
Still, the sea separates me. A few metres of rusty tide.
Head and tail near separate, the bend of a broken limb.
The people come. This unusual spectacle from the belly
of our waters vomited onto the shore. *You can smell it*
before you see it. The council best come with a JCB.
Long ago, the head would be cracked open. Oil a blessing
in such a place, where land and people were flensed by famine.
Without context, I would straddle him. Clamp my heels
as to a mare, or man. If only I could plead ignorance
of proprietary and rot. Is this an urge to dominate,
or to feel buoyancy, the weightless depths I can't know?

They do things differently there

This is a project of excavation. History. How these boats went to the deep and tore their prey apart on land.

This is not a story about the present. The whale populations have been depleted for so long.

What would anyone know now, of whales, here?

I spend more time on the internet. Curled in the armchair by the bookcase. A sedentary beast. The winter is wet and mild. The spring, wet and cold.

After the sperm whale washed in from the deep, I think we just got lucky. Or him unlucky. The whales are gone, or at the very least, so far out to sea that they'd only be spotted if you knew where to look, if you were on a deep-sea trawler or research vessel. I know so little about whales.

'Did you know there are still whales in Irish waters?' I shout to Mariner. I am scanning pages about species, numbers, sighting records.

A map shows good spots to watch from.

Hours on clifftops with binoculars.

Like stargazing for comets,

waiting for that unlikely high.

Where are the women?

In reading so much about whaling, I am thinking about capitalism, about the patriarchy. The usual suspects. The drive for extraction of a resource, for accumulation of capital, of power. The reduction of the animals into nothing more than a resource. It's easy, as a woman, to read, to feel outraged without feeling culpable.

Now, I am sending my man to sea.

However, separating the male-centred industry from women is an easy out. Women were present on whaling boats. Wives of captains were known to come along, for either economic reasons or to be with their husbands. Wives left behind were breadwinners and heads of households.

Richard Ellis notes that 'Men did the hunting, the killing, the flensing, the sailing, the drowning, the dying. But it might be said that much of it was done *for* women.'[46]

In the 19th and early 20th centuries, whalebone corsets were popular in fashion. The whalebone from which they were made was not bone at all, but the keratin baleen used to filter their food. It was a pliable but strong material that made it perfect for corsets. It was also used in buggies, hoop skirts, umbrellas and other such uses which have since been replaced by plastic.

I find an early twentieth-century advertisement for corsets shows a woman holding a box with the inscription, 'A WOMAN HAS AN AWFUL LOT TO THANK A WHALE FOR'[47].

Which is true. Whale oil was also used in soap and cosmetics. Ambergris from the gut of the sperm whale is extremely valuable for use in perfume. The body of the whale was used to decorate the female body, a fact many historians put weight on.

At a time when women did not yet have the vote, couldn't inherit property, and numerous other economic and political inequalities, a woman had an awful lot to thank her beauty for.

I sit uncomfortably with the fact that, born in another time, I would have worn whale gut fragrance as readily as I wear leather boots. Still, I wouldn't have killed a whale, I tell myself. Surely, I'd never have lusted after the hunt.

When will my love return from sea?

I burst into the bedroom before the sun.

'Two questions, what are you doing next week, and do you trust me?'

He raises an eyebrow, then smiles.

We're not going to see whales from the land. We'd need binoculars, the right weather, and the one thing we definitely don't have: hours. We have a child and bills. The cost of oil more than doubled this winter. Our recent electric bill cost more than a month's rent when I was in college. Our days are spent earning. The transaction of time is ever-crystallising.

Where we put our time, our money, has to be carefully chosen.

'I'm not sure we can afford it,' he says.

'It's an investment.' I say it like every desire-addled addict.

There's been a last-minute opening on the *Celtic Mist*, the IWDG's boat used to survey Irish waters for cetaceans. As a mother of a young child, being at sea for several nights is not possible, but Mariner will sail for me. Ahab by proxy.

I drop him to the train which will bring him to the port. The car sputters fumes as I idle in the set-down spot.

'Bring me home a whale,' I say as he bends to kiss me through the open window.

IMMRAM MIOLBHÁDORÍ
Mariner as Watcher

The VHF sizzles into garbled life, storm warnings, distress calls, damage reports from across the bay and further out-shushed by a southerly's cool bite. Poolbeg Quay glints through slow cumuli and the rusty cranes at half-mast are like wilted obelisks, salivating with sunlight as it slants and kindles. Through my cabin's starboard porthole is Alexandria Basin, the warm push of tides still untroubled by a prow. We'll be underway soon.

If you long for water, the price will be in salt. From playschool through to college and beyond, from milk bottle to pint glass, the sea frosted at the back of my head like an incomplete task, a sun-whisked keepsake. Legends of krakens and ghost ships, so cosily terrifying, still hook me; visions of condemned miscreants left to sway eerily in a sea breeze swirl through my dreams. As the years passed, such phantasmagoria gave way to the vital science of sailor's knots, the reading of tidal shifts, bearing-taking, depth-sounding, mile-measurement and log entry, the boredom of the open ocean, the very real menace of storms. But I've neither the mariner's hard-won instinct for sudden shifts in weather nor the angler's serenity for standing watch in wait of a tug on his line, or a helmsman's skill for laying a course and vessel manoeuvre.

In a previous life, the *Mist* was a former Taoiseach's luxury yacht. She's since been refitted accordingly as a research vessel. The burgundy-tinged logbook remains perched in her wheelhouse, Haughey's elegant, spidery scrawl blackening its pages. Anacharsis's unproven saying clangs in the ear: all who are at sea may be ranked neither with the living nor the dead, and only four fingers shall keep death at a remove, four fingers equalling the density of a ship's rib and chassis.

I have plundered the lives of those more adventurous than I for long enough, their obsessions becoming mine, fleshed out to the palest detail, their declarations repeated to the most slender syllable, a mind drenched in boyhood's nostalgic sheen. Triremes with throbbing eyes tinted on prows, sweeping the sun-fevered Aegean for a city of horse-breaking princes and Trojan doom, the arms of thunder locking over sand, thalassic ash rolling in every throat. Crumpled paper, blade-shaped sails, the crew's imperilled roar as a white broadside, caused by the boulder lobbed by the eyeless giant from his tall headland, buffeted stern and prow, waves churning like fiendish oil, their dark bubbles retching in a sash of ermine surf. Flags fully raised, Pirate Republics flying a black collage of skeleton, hourglass, bayonet.

Blood given the shape of diamonds. Ship, sea and shore, my atomic world still turning like a page; men, women, who burned holes in the world's fabric, all ashes now for the wind's apathy to sweep up. They're not much to come home to nor much to show my son, these crude drawings of ships I'd scribbled as a boy, each dusty colour veering wildly out of the line. A magnet pinioned one of them to the fridge door.

Life-jacketed, boots planted to the deck, I stand to the fore where the wind feels full-frontal on all sides as our ketch skims mulishly southward, opaque and terrestrial on the rim of dawn. At last, we're underway! A swell of elation brews. After a life spent admiring, reading and trying my hand at writing of the sea, at last, I'm on the verge of my old vision. All such dreams that I once harboured, I stand at the helm of now: undulating blue-green that encircles our hull, the potent sting of surf on the deck rail.

Wearing the costume of what was hammered into the skull from the schoolyard up: work, earn, provide, stand tall: wear that husbandly and fatherly fatigue of another week-long chase.

I'm away from her and our son. Being away from either of them for any stretch of time tends to wear me down, leaves me feeling incomplete and unmoored. I'll be home to them soon, but our boy is at an age where a week may as well be an eternity. I snap photos and send them whenever the signal picks up. She once told me her first true sense of being an adult came when she learned to drive. Mine came from being her lover, becoming a father to her son.

Their absence gives me pause to remember it will not be years or even a months-long sojourn, but a mere week before the mast for me, keeping well inshore, both passenger and crew member.

On deck, we move in a shared cadence as our eyes strain against spray spattering the hull, cooling our cheeks. Slow-going, and yet we know no boredom, for there is none in standing watch, lost to the horizon, eyes locked on crests weaving and seething into a flux of spindrift like ceaseless brushstrokes. I could scan for a millennium, the hours slipping by unheeded yet hinged on the ship, never to grace the same waters twice. An early sun will soon scorch the fog off like jetsam, and we'll steer each other through a swell-choked Dublin Bay, past the Muglins and Dalkey Sound, hold fast against this high breeze from far above the equator, not as hunters, but as mere observers. We don't pursue as Ahab did, enmeshed always in the chase.

Everyone aboard takes turns steering, though the less experienced, like myself, defer to those more skilled. Sea-spray mists our skin. I cannot deny the way the blue span carries us, its swells like a procession of liquid giants swaying us along a passage awash with the pleasure of movement as we ride their rolling backs, lathers of spray spat in our faces as we pass the firm bluff of Wicklow, Arklow's sandbank where wind turbines twirl like iron feathers, slashing the air in blurry acceleration. We relieve each other of duty, stand in chilly watch, eye the to and fro of ripples and crests as if a humpback might breach the surface. We call out whatever we see.

Our radar might detect whisperings in the abyss, grace notes in crackled reverb, depth charges garbling the wireless in a chamber choir of undersea sonics, curbing the velocity of our minor ark to dead slow as coffee from a flask sloshes in my throat like surf on a porthole.

Harbour lights marshal like a platoon of glow worms as we make our berth at Kinsale, the Bandon sluicing through marinas for the estuary where Spanish sails once bellied in somnolent fore, carracks and galleons and black welters eddying to gild our waterline in rust. I eyeball the dark, note the radar's bleep. Were it not for her, I wouldn't be aboard this ship. Were it not for her, very little would have taken place. I am here because they lured her — the whales. In her name, I keep a weather eye out for their slow swim, worship what I may hunt, and all without the aim of killing or taking a prize. The whales may yet surface, as the wind picks up. 'Til then, I'll catch the stars when I can.

Fishes royal

Mariner sails from Dublin to Kinsale. It's the right time of year, but the whales aren't making an appearance. If they're not there, where are they?

Irish humpbacks could be seen in the waters of West Cork and Kerry. Sea safaris and dedicated boats brought tourists out to spy for whales.

Until recently, when the season rolled round and the whales weren't showing.

But they were still here. They'd moved north.

I'm on Instagram, scrolling, when I see the boat. I followed the account to visit Inishkea. Someone tags them. There are photos.

'Look at this,' I say to Mariner, 'she's here, in Mayo.' I am giddy.

Humpback 67, or Queen Medb, was the first humpback I'd heard of in Irish waters. Named after the Irish warrior queen, HB67 is recognisable by the scars on her left fluke which indicate a battle with an orca.

Members of the Irish Whale and Dolphin Group have gone out to record her. My feed is flooded with images of her, her open jaws, her tail slapping the water, her striped belly arched against the horizon.

She's out there.

I send a lot of emails. I want to get on that boat. There are no public whale watching boats in Mayo. The boats operating in the area are primarily fishing, research, or island tours. I am directed, politely, to the cliffs.

Watcher as hiker

Aching with impatience, I see something.

A vertical wave. A spit of spray. One rounded black curve.

Head or back, a second glance would tell. But from this height, my children's monocular loses whatever it was, or wasn't. A trick of the eye. Longing revealing itself. Like all those feared or wished for ghosts, sheet white in hallways.

Come on, you fuckers, show yourselves

How quickly something wanted, but untouchable, becomes the enemy.

I have been here before. Possessed by want; one sharp point

in focus, the rest of the world only sea mist.

I am vicious with pursuit and disappointment. Sick with myself.

Doesn't every woman know what it is to be wanted?

Wanted wanted wanted.

Until moving is intolerable

and she'd throw herself on the harpoon.

In its capture the thing you have been seeking ceases to exist.

The water moves with only waves.

A poster of a corncrake drawn by a child

On top of Erris Head, grumpy from seeing nothing but waves, I turn for the car. The Atlantic wind and roaming sheep keep flora knee-high at best. There's no sound but waves and wind, no birdsong or leaves rustling, so it is easy to catch the *crex crex* coming from a few metres inland. I've never heard it in real life, but it cuts across the years and I'm back at school learning about the national campaign to save the corncrakes. I imagined them as the next dodo. I sobbed when the harvester would rip through the meadow next door. It felt like living among the dinosaurs and watching a comet fall slowly to earth.

In the 1960s, there was a population of 4,000 corncrakes in Ireland. By the new millennium, the numbers were as low as 100. Mechanised farming, in particular the mowing of fields from the edges towards the middle of the field, leaving the corncrakes with nowhere to run, was thought to be the primary cause of this rapid decline.

I quickly find the sound on YouTube and play it to see if I recognise the call correctly. No sooner have I pressed play than the bird repeats its croak. Two birds together: one on my phone, looping indefinitely, one here, in this field, invisible to me but unmistakable. The corncrake.

A total of 218 corncrake breeding territories were recorded in 2023, up by 10 percent on 2022 and exceeding 200 for the first time in a decade.

In 1966, the International Whaling Commission banned the hunting of the humpback whale. Global numbers were estimated to be as low as 5,000 individual animals.

By 2018, their numbers had reached 135,000 worldwide.

135,000

Interview with Conor Ryan

Conor Ryan is a zoologist by trade. He splits his time between academia, conservation, education, and wildlife guiding. His research on cetaceans initially focused on environmental chemistry, but later, passive acoustics.

His paper, 'Insights into the biology and ecology of whales in Ireland 100 years ago from archived whaling data', was published in *The Irish Naturalists' Journal* in 2022.

Roots

My name is Conor Ryan. I grew up in Cobh near Cork, but I live on the Isle of Mull in Scotland.

I almost feel guilty that my subject matter is an easy sell. I think of people doing frog or newt conservation and people are like, 'Ew, they're cold and squishy. I don't like them,' whereas people automatically like whales.

My interest in them is to use them as a gateway drug to get people interested in ecology and the environment and to care a bit more. I think the whaling story in history is an amazing example of somewhere we can shake people up and say, 'Look, this is not normal. What it's like out there is not what it was like in the past and what it could be again.'

I grew up right by the sea. My father and cousin were in the navy when I was a kid. Whenever they would come back from sea, I'd quiz them on what they'd seen. If they'd seen no whales, I'd be really frustrated. If they hadn't looked, I'd be even more frustrated. This idea that there was something out there that could be seen if you'd just put the time in really amazed me.

When I was about ten, I made a new friend, Peter. His father is Jim Wilson, a keen ornithologist and natural historian. He'd take us out to headlands, and we'd sit all day, eating pot noodles and just watching the sea. He taught me how to keep notebooks. Those notebooks are still my most cherished possessions. If the house was on fire, I'd run for the notebooks!

When I was 15, killer whales came in in front of my house. We spent the whole summer following the whales on our bikes. We monitored their behaviour, taking notes in the notebooks we'd learned to take on the headland watches. We kept notes and published it as a paper. I didn't know the significance of this until I went to college. That really gave me a leg up.

I was surrounded by people who encouraged me to take interest in wildlife and nature. People could see how buzzed I was. I always wanted to be a whale biologist. At the time there weren't any in Ireland. It was a pie in the sky idea, but I was allowed the opportunity and it worked out.

Education in Ireland was free. If it wasn't, I don't know if I'd have had such free reign to go and take those risks to pursue something like zoology and specialise in whales.

Whale watching

When I started getting into whales, I saved enough money to buy a moped so I could go up to headlands. I'd drive for three hours on this moped to Galley Head and sit on a headland. Every time there was an observation, this was new information: where did the fin and humpback whales come from? What time of year did they come? Why are they here? How do we facilitate their recovery? I found the whole process quite addictive, really. I was involved with the IWDG and they were getting the word out there, that we have these whales in Ireland. You don't have to go far to see them.

I was interested in the skill of field identification; how do we know if it's a sei whale rather than a fin whale, for example. In college I went on state research vessels and saw sperm whales, pilot whales. I went to West Africa during my PhD to see the humpback whales there, gradually expanding to the Southern Ocean, which is whale mecca.

Most of the whales in Ireland stay in the northern hemisphere. The whales I see in the south are on a sort of opposite shift. In Cape Verde, you get humpbacks from both hemispheres, but rarely at the same time. They move six months apart. This was one of the things I described in more detail by using their song to define separate populations.

Humpbacks are making a big recovery. Blue whales are too, but the verdict is out on the size of that recovery. They're being spotted places they haven't for years, such as South Georgia. There's also Antarctic minke whales and right whales in South Georgia and the Falkland Islands. Right whales are gone from Ireland. People go down to the beach to watch them. We lost that. No, it was taken from us, the ability to watch them from our beaches, but it's a glimpse of what could have been, or maybe what could be. There are North Atlantic right whales off the USA and Canada, and there's always a small chance they could expand and recolonise Ireland.

Irish whaling

When I was doing my PhD, I was so focused on field work, I didn't really give enough thought to what happened in the past. History used to bore me. I couldn't see the relevance. I've matured out of that. Before I submitted my PhD, Jim Wilson gave me a copy of James Fairley's book. That was the only source about Irish whaling at that time.

During Covid was when I started to take it seriously. I wanted to do some analysis or data mining, to increase awareness.

Why have some species recovered and some have not?

There are several things coming together. At the most fundamental level, the life history of these whales is slightly different. Humpbacks have a shorter lifespan and can produce a higher number of calves. They're more productive than other species. They were also protected at an earlier stage; they were given international special protection. Hunting of the right whale was banned in 1937. They were already commercially extinct. It was a last-ditch attempt to stop them going extinct. It failed for the right whales and seemed to have worked for the humpbacks.

Humpbacks have a wider diet, they're more adaptable. Fin, sei, and right whales prefer zooplankton, namely krill and copepods.. What is happening with the plankton affects the whales. What I don't understand is that some species like basking sharks are recovering, and they're zoo plankton specialists, but some of the bigger species just aren't.

There could be factors such as being hunted elsewhere. There's been an exposé of illegal Soviet whaling. They were whaling covertly all over the world after it was banned, though no one scrutinises the Dutch, the Spanish, the English with the same intensity. We may yet find records that other species were being hunted unbeknownst to us.

Humpback whales are showing signs of recovery. I wouldn't have said that even five years ago, but that's what the evidence is showing now.

Risks

What motivates the whales to come to Ireland is food. If we can't protect their prey, they won't come back. The marine institute estimates how many fish are in the sea around Ireland. The herring and sprat need to be there in such abundance that the whales can't eat all of it. If females bring their calves to Ireland, that will imprint on them, and they'll bring their offspring.

We also need to stop accidentally killing them. Entanglement in lobster pots, prawn pots. It's happening enough here in Scotland that it's preventing recovery. For humpback whales, the number of entanglements in Scotland are comparable to those during the peak of the shore-based whaling there. It is likely the same in Ireland. We've replaced whaling with entanglement.

Whale watching

There's always a risk we could love them to death. Whale-watching on a small scale is fine, but if it's not managed it can damage them due to physical and acoustic disturbance. In Iceland, there's a frightening number of boats trying to get a view. They're filling the whales' world with noise and risking hitting them. The worst whale watching experience I had was in New Zealand, looking at sperm whales. It's mass tourism on poor whales just trying to get a rest between deep dives.

The weather usually keeps the numbers down in Ireland. The government needs to be proactive in management before it becomes a problem.

For the whales to be worth more alive than dead is a good way to help them to recover, but how much noise is too much for them? The balance is the key. Whale-watching does seem to be growing. It used to be West Cork or nowhere, but it has spread around, and so have the whales.

Watcher as internet lurker

Humpback whale, Doughmakeon, Mayo, 23 June 2023

Another summer storm is rolling in. The wind is hot, Clare Island a hazy silhouette. Tyre tracks: we've missed it. The council come to sink it in sand or haul it back to sea. The birds clue me in. Small and far away. We walk, steadier than before, the tide on our side. The smell. Fish, and the zoo. Not rot as I'd expect, but an oceanic burp.

And here it is,

this quintessential whale, like a child's toy. Waxy. A remarkable likeness to the rubber whales, piled in plastic drawers beside rubber camels, octopus, elephants, tapir, sheep. How unreal it seems.

Tubercles. Rings left by barnacles like mug rings on the desk.

Its corrugated throat collapsed in on itself, deflated. I think of the hollow of my breasts, now, when lying flat on my back, like parts of me are falling away inside myself, but I digress.

All up the tail are footprints.

Its eye, or should I say his. His lids rounded and clasped to close. Plump around the slit, like a freshly waxed vulva. I want to pull them apart, just there, a whale eye. The set of the mouth holding baleen, plates of it, I see the once valuable elements of the body, as if the whalers from the books were starting to seep into me.

The skin peeling away like flakes of wallpaper. Black, just black. Beneath it, bleached.

Any one could be *the* white whale, stripped enough.

A family come along, take photos, two children posing. The father kicks the carcass with his welly. I bite away the tut of disrespect. Am I any different?

Is this a site of mourning or the natural order of things?

No, none of this can be natural, not anymore. How humans have disrupted the ebb and flow of it.

That is, unless we zoom out. Temporally.

See the invasive species swarm and overflow, colonise and overexploit, starve itself, break down, recede, vanish.

Slowly

order resumes.

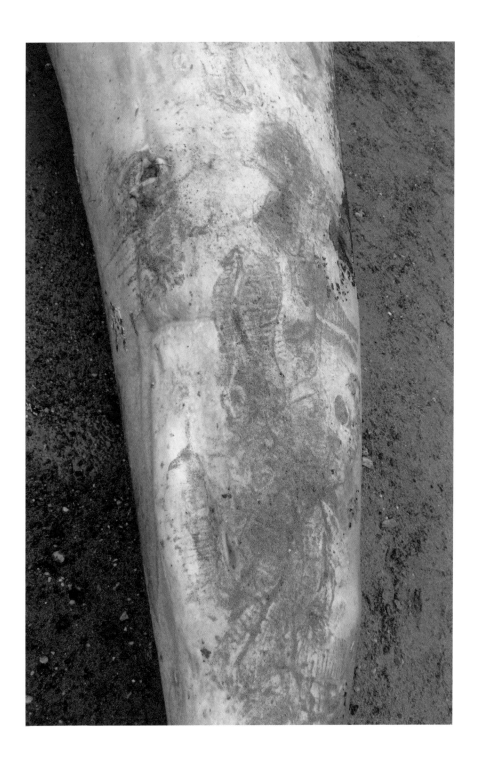

SAVE THE WHALES

'Whales are a renewable resource and could have continued if the figures supplied by scientists had not been ignored by some whaling operators or stretched by politicians beyond all reasonable tolerances.'[48]

We know that petrol didn't save the whale, yet few people now think of whales as a resource. At some point, conservation of whaling became the conservation of whales themselves. What we now know about cetaceans is incomparable to the public opinion of whales in centuries gone by. We know that whales are complex social animals. They live in families, communicate through intricate sounds that have remarkable similarities to human languages. The empathy that the public feels towards these animals has arisen due to the increased information about them. The idea of whales as creatures worthy of empathy became popular in the latter half of the 20th century. A confluence of circumstances is behind this.

Sea/world

The increased ease with which cetaceans could be captured due to the technological developments of the late 19th and early 20th centuries meant that they could not only be killed with ease, they could be captured *alive*. While the large whales such as humpbacks are too big, orcas and dolphins became attractions in SeaWorld and other aquariums worldwide.

This began in the 1860s, when two beluga whales were caught and displayed in New York in Barnum's American Museum. Others across the US and Europe followed, with dolphins and belugas dying rapidly in small tanks.

The first bottlenose dolphin to be trained was in Florida's Marine Studios. In the 1960s, the release of the *Flipper* series popularised captive cetaceans. The practice of capturing orcas for aquariums and public entertainment began in the same decade. Whales were caught off Puget Sound, and later Iceland.

People had been getting close to whales for centuries in the ocean, but whales in captivity meant people could see whales not just in photographs, or dead on a beach. They could see them in what was presented as their 'natural habitat' – water – while of course there was nothing natural at all about cetaceans swimming in large glass pools.

The 2010 documentary *Blackfish* unearthed some of the horrors of orcas in captivity following the death of an experienced SeaWorld trainer. An orca's lifespan in captivity is approximately half that of in the wild. Male orcas' dorsal fins collapse in captivity. One whale, the largest to be held in captivity, was responsible for the deaths of three trainers.

As of 2024, 56 Orcas remain in captivity.

Song

Hydrophones that had been developed for tools of war found an alternative use in their detection of the sounds of whales. In 1967, American biologist Roger Payne discovered whale song among humpbacks. He used hydrophones that had been previously used to listen out for Soviet submarines. Payne's research proved that humpback whales did not just make random sounds. They sang. They used rhyme, repetition, structure, to communicate. Speech, something so human, was a part of the whales too. The public was beginning to understand that whales were intelligent creatures with complex family relationships that were capable of creating music.

In 1970, Payne released an LP of recordings called *Songs of the Humpback Whale*. It was an unexpected hit, selling over 125,000 copies and going multi-platinum. It received the support of artists such as Bob Dylan and Joan Baez. Numerous sources published information about the threats to these beloved creatures. Developments in film technology, especially underwater cameras and the household television, brought whales into people's living rooms. In 1977, *National Geographic* aired The Great Whales, which featured scenes with whales being killed. Documentaries by David Attenborough and Jacque Cousteau furthered public awareness around the lives of whales.

Bumper stickers and t-shirts declaring 'Save the Whales' became popular through organisations such as Greenpeace. Greenpeace's activities included Project Ahab, where activists physically blocked the harpoons of whalers. The phrase was also used in in 1977 when a 14-year-old girl, Maris Sidenstecker, learning of the danger to the whales, designed a t-shirt and found herself quickly inundated with orders. Sidenstecker and her mother founded Save the Whales, a non-profit organisation which still operates today.

In 1979, *National Geographic* sent an extract of *Songs of the Humpback Whale* to its 10.5 million subscribers.

Artists, scientists, activists, and the public caused pressure to mount on an international scale.

Success, sort of

Commercial whaling was banned in 1986. While the initial moratorium on whaling came about to preserve whale stocks, its development to the protection of whales we know today was primarily influenced by the international public pressure of the Save the Whales movement. Whales went from being *beasts*, a resource, to being a beloved image of marine life. Now, they are the stuff of cuddly toys and boating tours, or the *I whaley love you* photo frame my son bought me for my birthday.

It was this affection for whales behind the public pressure that cemented the moratorium. The whales were, to an extent, saved. If it can be done for whales, can't it be done for us?

I wonder whether public pressure would have been sufficient if the industry had still been immensely profitable.

Blasket Encounter[49]

On Easter Monday morning, April 12th 1982, we weighed anchor at Portmagee harbour and set sail for the Blasket Islands, some 20 miles to the north. We were a group of six friends from Cork on a cruising holiday on the southwest coast. Our boat was a 36 foot ketch, chartered in Bantry where we had departed from the previous day.

The day was glorious. The sea was slight, and the breeze was a gentle force 3 on the beam. We reached the Blasket archipeligo shortly after noon and spent a few delectable hours sailing amongst the islands. On approaching Inishvickillane island we were hailed from the cliff top and invited ashore "for tea" by the owner, Charles Haughey, who was spending his Easter vacation on the island. We anchored in eight fathoms in the bight at the north side of the island and proceeded ashore in the dinghy.

somehow there was something vaguely familiar about the sounds. I racked my brains. Then it came to me. I was listening to the song of a Humpback whale. Some years previously National Geographic magazine published an article by zoologist Roger Payne on the singing habits of the Humpback. The magazine had supplied a sound record of some of Roger's Humpback whale song recording. I had idly played this record a few times, prompted more by curiosity than any particular interest in the subject. Then I had forgotton all about it, until now. At this stage I had to convince myself that I was actually awake and not dreaming, or hearing Charlies "tea". I awakened Vivienne, one of the crew and together we listened, enthralled, to this symphony of the deep for the best part of half an hour.

The remainder of our cruise passed off very pleasantly, but my experience that night triggered a whole series of questions. I wondered how I

It was late evening when we disengaged from the very welcome, if unexpected, hospitality afforded us on Inishvickillane. As we made our way back to the anchorage I noted that the wind had dropped to nothing. It wasn't just a local condition as I could see smoke from gorse fires in the distance on the mainland rising vertically. The sea was now calm as a millpond. Our original intention had been to press on to Dingle. Now, given the very rare set of circumstances which would permit a comfortable anchorage in the Blaskets, we decided to forego the fleshpots of Dingle and stay put for the night. I was delighted. It had been an ambition of mine to spend a night in what the 'South and West' cruising guide describes as the "loneliest anchorage in the world". We discussed the events of the day and the plans for the morrow over a very pleasant meal and turned in.

About 2 a.m. I awoke to hear a strange, mournful, eerie, wailing sound. The piteous moans reverberated like they were emanating from a vast echo chamber. It was surreal. I had just awakened from a deep sleep and I was struggling to make sense of what I was hearing. I knew that I had never heard anything like this at sea before, but

could have heard underwater sounds at all. I was aware from my reading of the Blasket literature of the "fairy music" of Inishvickillane. Could there be a possible connection? This fairy music was supposed to be the inspiration of a traditional air "Port na bPucai", literally translated "the ghostly tune". I had never heard the tune. When I did hear it, would it bear any resemblance to the sounds I heard that night?

I re-read Roger Payne's article and anything else I could lay my hands on regarding the subject. Lo, it transpired that, yes, underwater sounds could be transmitted through the hull of a boat. In fact, in the era of the sailing ships, before engines, sailors were well accustomed to hearing the sounds of whales and dolphins through the hulls of their ships. I turned my attention now to the literature and the legends. Robin Flower, an English scholar who developed a deep affinity with the Blasket Islanders during the early part of this century wrote of his experiences in his book "The Western Island". In it he relates one story of the origin of Port na bPucai.

In the old days, when the island was inhabited, a man sat alone one night in his house, soothing his loneliness with a fiddle. He was playing, no doubt, the favourite music of the countryside, jigs and reels and hornpipes, the hurrying tunes that would put light heels on the feet of the dead. But, as he played, he heard another music without, going over the roof in the air. It passed away to the cliffs and returned again, and so backwards and forwards again and again, a wandering air wailing in repeated phrases, till at last it had become familiar in his mind, and he took up the fallen bow, and drawing it across the strings followed note by note the lamentiing voices as they passed above him. Ever since, that tune, port na bpucai, "the fairy music", has remained with his family, skilled musicians all, and, if you hear it played by a fiddler of that race, you will know the secret of Inisicileain.

I had difficulty reconciling the legend with my own experience. Inisvickillane is a high island and I could not explain how underwater sounds, however intense, could be heard so far above the surface of the sea.

The search continued. In the music section of Cork city library I located an L.P. by traditional fiddler Tommy Peoples which featured Port na bPucai. As I listened to Tommy's unaccompanied plaintive rendition of the tune I heard, with excitement, familiar twists and phrases in the music which were evocative of the Payne recordings and what I had recalled hearing myself in the Blaskets. But now I made an unexpected discovery. The sleeve notes on Tommy Peoples L.P. had a piece written by Tony McMahon, himself a noted traditional musician, which gave a different version of the Port na bPucai legend. Tony's version puts three Inishvickillane men in a currach returning home from a ceili on the Great Blasket Island. It was a calm moonlit night. While at sea they heard the strange music. One of the three was a fiddler and he played along with the music thereby absorbing the tune. I was now quite excited. This version of the legend was compatible with my own experience. It was a boat at sea. The currach would have been approaching the landing place near where we were anchored. Their night was calm as was ours. For a traditional musician to pick up a strange tune by ear would not be considered extraordinary. It was then and still remains the normal method of passing on traditional music.

I have discussed my experience with authorities on traditional music. I learnt that Sean O'Rioda was intrigued by the tune and sought to determine its origins but without coming to any conclusion. In relating my story I detected a slight resentment at the explaining away of a legend. This is a pity. I know that it is a lovely concept that such a wonderful tune might have come to us from the parallel supernatural world of the fairies. I think that it is no less lovely a concept that this tune might also have come from the parallel natural community of the oceans - the great whales.

Eugene O'Malley

Text reads:

Blasket Encounter

On Easter Monday morning, April 12th 1982, we weighed anchor at
Portmagee harbour and set sail for the Blasket Islands, some 20 miles to the
north. We were a group of six friends from Cork on a cruising holiday on
the southwest coast. Our boat was a 36 foot ketch, chartered in Bantry
where we had departed from the previous day.

The day was glorious. The sea was slight, and the breeze was a gentle force 3
on the beam. We reached the Blasket archipeligo shortly after noon and
spent a few deflectable hours sailing amongst the islands. On approaching
Inishvickillane island we were hailed from the cliff top and invited ashore
"for tea" by the owner, Charles Haughey, who was spending his Easter
vacation on the island. We anchored in eight fathoms in the bight at the
north side of the island and proceeded ashore in the dinghy. It was late
evening when we disengaged from the very welcome, if unexpected,
hospitality afforded us on Inishvickillane. As we made our way back to the
anchorage I noted that the wind had dropped to nothing. It wasn't just a
local condition as I could see smoke from gorse fires in the distance on the
mainland rising vertically. The sea was now calm as a millpond. Our original
intention had been to press on to Dingle. Now, given the very rare set of
circumstances which would permit a comfortable anchorage in the Blaskets,
we decided to forego the fleshpots of Dingle and stay put for the night. I
was delighted. It had been an ambition of mine to spend a night in what
the 'South and West' cruising guide describes as the "loneliest anchorage in
the world". We discussed the events of the day and the plans for the
morrow over a very pleasant meal and turned in.

About 2 a.m. I awoke to hear a strange, mournful, eerie, wailing sound. The
piteous moans reverberated like they were emanating from a vast echo
chamber. It was surreal. I had just awakened from a deep sleep and I was
struggling to make sense of what I was hearing. I knew that I had never
heard anything like this at sea before, but somehow there was something
vaguely familiar about the sounds. I racked my brains. Then it came to me. I
was listening to the song of a Humpback whale. Some years previously
National Geographic magazine published an article by zoologist Roger Payne
on the singing habits of the Humpback. The magazine had supplied a
sound record of some of Roger's Humpback whale song recording. I had
idly played this record a few times, prompted more by curiosity than any
particular interest in the subject. Then I had forgotten all about it, until now.
At this stage I had to convince myself that I was actually awake and not

dreaming, or hearing Charlie's "tea". I awakened Vivienne, one of the crew and together we listened, enthralled, to this symphony of the deep for the best part of half an hour. The remained of our cruise passed off very pleasantly, but my experience that night triggered a whole series of questions. I wondered how I could have heard underwater sounds at all. I was aware from my reading of the Blasket literature of the "fairy music" of Inishvickillaine. Could there be a possible connection? This fairy music was supposed to be the inspiration of a traditional air "Port na bPúcaí", literally translated "the ghostly tune". I had never heard the tune. When I did hear it, would it bear any resemblance to the sounds I heard that night? I re-read Roger Payne's article and anything else I could lay my hands on regarding the subject. Lo, it transpired that , yes, underwater sounds could be transmitted through the hull of a boat. In fact, in the era of the sailing ships, before engines, sailors were well accustomed to hearing the sounds of whales and dolphins through the hulls of their ships. I turned my attention now to the literature and the legends. Robin Flower, an English scholar who developed a deep affinity with the Blasket Islanders during the early part of this century wrote of his experiences in his book "The Western Island". In it he relates one story of the origin of Port na bPúcaí.

In the old days, when the island was inhabited, a man sat alone one night in his house, soothing his loneliness with a fiddle. He was playing, no doubt, the favourite music of the countryside, jigs, and reels and hornpipes, the hurrying tunes that would put light heels on the feet of the dead. But, as he played, he heard another music without, going over the roof in the air. It passed away to the cliffs and returned again, and so backwards and forwards again and again, a wandering air wailing in repeated phrases, till at last it had become familiar in his mind, and he took up the fallen bow, and drawing it across the strings followed note by note the lamenting voices as they passed above him. Ever since, that tune, Port na bPúcaí, "the fairy music", has remained with his family, skilled musicians all, and if you hear it played by a fiddler of that race, you will know the secret of Inisvickillane.

I had difficulty reconciling the legend with my own experience. Inisvickillane is a high island and I could not explain how underwater sounds, however intense, could be heard so far above the surface of the sea.

The search contined. In the music section of Cork city library I located an L.P. by traditional fiddler Tommy Peoples which featured Port na bPúcaí. As I listened to Tommy's unaccompanied plaintive rendition of the tune I heard, with excitement, familiar twists and phrases in the music which were evocative of the Payne recordings and what I had recalled hearing myself in the Blaskets. But now I made an unexpected discovery. The sleeve notes on Tommy Peoples' L.P. had a piece written by Tony McMahon, himself a noted traditional musician, which gave a different version of the Port na bPúcaí legend. Tony's version puts three Inishvickillane men in a currach returning home from a ceili on the Great Blasket Island. It was a calm moonlit night. While at sea they heard the strange music. One of the three was a fiddler and he played along with the music thereby absorbing the tune. I was now quite excited. This version of the legend was compatible with my own experience. It was a boat at sea. The currach would have been approaching the landing place near where we were anchored. Their neight was calm as was ours. For a traditional musician to pick up a strange tune by ear would not be considered extraordinary. It was then and still remains the normal method of passing on traditional music.

I have discussed my experience with authorities on traditional music. I learnt that Seán Ó Riada was intrigued by the tune and sought to determine its origins but without coming to any conclusion. In relating my story I detected a slight resentment at the explaining away of a legend. This is a pity. I know that it is a lovely concept that such a wonderful tune might have come to us from the parallel supernatural world of the fairies. I think that it is no less lovely a concept that this tune might also have come from the parallel natural community of the oceans – the great whales.

– Eugene O'Malley

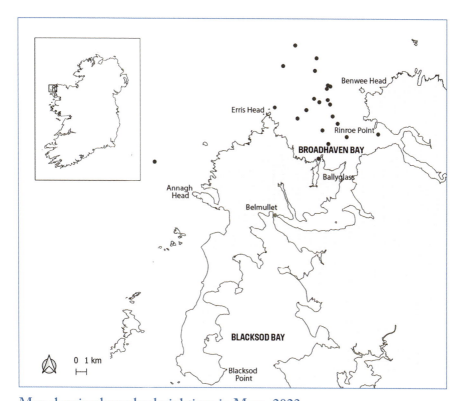

Map showing humpback sightings in Mayo, 2023.
Data provided by the Irish Whale and Dolphin Group. Map: Éadaoin Ní Néill

MAYO WHALE AND DOLPHIN SURVEY[50]

June 1993 off the Mullet Peninsula

Song of the Whale research vessel

none of the species of large whale that were caught
between 1908-1922 were observed during the survey

The lack of large whale sightings

may have been influenced by poor sea conditions or

their overall absence in the area.

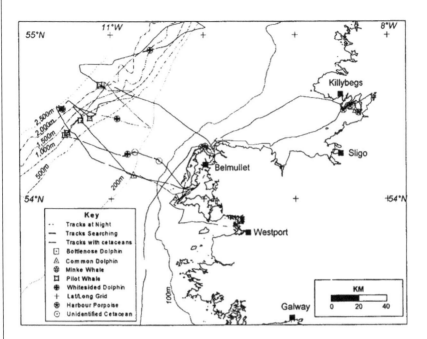

Figure 1. Location of cetacean sightings and survey tracks off Mayo and Donegal during June and July 1993.

Watcher as thwarted

Today, a *too fresh* turned sea. A boat shackled to harbour.

There'll be no return to Inishkea. A consolation walk,

binoculars clutched. Hours perched on a stye.

Watching, waiting. Hood up. Face slapped.

Patience *must* be rewarded. The sea a thousand spouts.

I watch. Gulls. Shags. The cliffs. Will hope give out?

Interview with Gemma O'Connor

Gemma is IWDG's live stranding coordinator. Originally from North Kerry, she now lives with her family on the Mullet Peninsula, County Mayo, which is one of Ireland's main hotspots for mass strandings of common dolphins.

Roots

I've always been interested in cetaceans. I grew up on a farm beside the sea in North Kerry and loved being out in a currach, fishing for mackerel, pollock, and lobsters. I had planned on studying marine biology at NUIG, but ended up studying and working in IT for years.

When I left Kerry I moved to Limerick, and while it was hard to leave the coast, I eventually got used to it. However, I always longed to return to the coast. I started working for my brother's company, hoping I would eventually be able to work remotely. About a year later, I moved to the Mullet Peninsula in Mayo. It was just like home but with a more diverse array of marine life. I had often encountered bottlenose dolphins in North Kerry, but here I was seeing common dolphins, basking sharks, minke whales, pelagic seabirds, and eventually, my first humpback whale. My desire to become actively involved with marine life and make a difference continued to grow.

I learned that the area was a hotspot for live strandings of common dolphins, with a few mass strandings occurring each year. At the time, locals and marine biologists would attend these stranding events and do what they could for the dolphins. Initially, I was working full-time, but over the years, my husband Cillian and I welcomed three children. As a result, it took a number of years before I got involved locally with live strandings.

One cold November day, I received a phone call about 11 common dolphins stranded in a known hotspot. I quickly realised that I was the only person in the area available to help, as the previous responders had moved away. I called friends to assist and called IWDG. IWDG provided training and shared as much information as possible with the new wave of volunteers on the Mullet Peninsula. Over time, IWDG started receiving more calls from all over Ireland about live stranded dolphins, especially with the rise of social media and increased public awareness of where to report strandings. It became clear that a live stranding coordinator was needed, and with my hands-on experience, I was delighted to get the role.

Curiosities

You never know what's going to come in on the other end of the phone. I once drove to Killybegs to give a live stranding course, and the phone rang. A man called and said his wife was on a remote beach with a harbour porpoise, and she was trying to refloat it. He wanted me to call her and reassure her that it was probably at the end of its life.

When I called her, I asked, 'Does it have a small dorsal fin? Is it a small animal? Does it have a beak? Where's the dorsal fin—halfway along its body or two-thirds back?' Something didn't sound right. She said, 'It has a very small mandible.' Was this even a harbour porpoise at all I wondered? I had her FaceTime me, and as soon as I saw the mouth, I realised she had a pygmy sperm whale. That animal shouldn't be here; it's a tropical water species. It was very thin and covered in lesions, which indicated it was severely unwell. Refloating it wasn't in the best interests of that little whale, so I explained this and asked her and the kids to stop their attempt. She agreed, and with nightfall approaching and the cold setting in, the best thing for them to do was walk away, which she did.

We tried to get a vet out there, but it was so remote, and darkness had fallen. NPWS arrived at first light, confirmed the little whale was deceased and they began the recovery of it from the area.

We wanted to get it for necropsy. IWDG was running a Deep Diving & Rare Species Investigation project, funded by NPWS, as the government doesn't currently run a cetacean necropsy scheme. This was the first recorded live pygmy sperm whale in Ireland. The necropsies are typically done in Regional Vet Labs, in Athlone, but this little whale was in Donegal, and it was summertime—it would bloat quickly. None of the volunteers could transport it, and I knew what was coming. I said, 'I'll do it.' NPWS arrived with the whale wrapped in plastic. It had been a beautiful pale blue, but by now, it was dark and covered in ink. Pygmy sperm whales have an ink sac that releases when they're stressed, and this one had released its ink, with the tide washing it all over its body. I stressed, 'It has to be really, really well wrapped, and the lab must be open for me tonight.' The whale was shoved into the back of my Volvo jeep, and with windows open, I left Killybegs for Athlone after the course. The head vet, on a Sunday, opened the lab at eight that night and took it in.

That was one of my strangest experiences. With global warming and rising sea temperatures, we now have a live tropical animal stranding in Ireland. We needed that postmortem to learn more about this species.

Queen Medb

I had been aware that humpbacks were starting to come to Mayo. I was checking IWDG's online sightings and noticed a report of a humpback breaching two miles west of Eagle Island. I mentioned it to our CEO, Simon Berrow, and he said, 'There's probably more, but no one is logging the sightings.' I decided to watch as much as I could and bought a spotting scope.

That summer, I received a text from Dave Suddaby about a humpback sighting off AMETS, the wave energy test site. There are only two buoys there collecting data. I went to Broadhaven the next day but saw nothing— not even a bird. Then, I went to Dún na mBó, near Eagle Island, and within an hour, I saw a minke whale, a humpback, and loads of dolphins. I was hooked.

The following year, I went to the cliffs and saw two humpbacks at Erris Head in early May. The humpbacks were arriving. I wondered, who are they? I visited the cliffs every evening to record sightings of the humpback that remained in Broadhaven to feed. I repeatedly asked around for a RIB to take me out and get an ID of these whales, but the summer boats weren't in the water, and the fishing boats were too busy catching mackerel. I was determined to get an ID and hoped to be lucky enough to get one from the cliff if the humpback came close enough.

One evening, I went to a headland in Broadhaven with my youngest child, and he suddenly said, 'Oh, look, I see the whale!' It was so close it looked as though the blows were coming up out of the grass. I immediately called my husband. I had my camera, a drone, and a seven-year-old on a cliff during strong winds, so my husband came to help. I tracked the whale around the headland while he launched the drone and managed to get a clear dorsal shot. Then, the whale fluked, and I captured a shot of the underside of her tail. It was so exciting—we were thrilled. After two weeks of trying to get out on a boat, we finally got the ID from the cliff. We found her ID on IWDG's humpback whale catalogue online, and Pádraig Whooley confirmed, 'Yes, you have her. That's #67.'

She has this habit: when she feeds, she comes up and keeps her head above the water. Whenever I was in town, I'd quickly head up to a cliff to look out, see a blow, and think, *that's her*. She stayed around for a few weeks, and then she was gone.

Irish Whale and Dolphin Group at work, Fin whale, Ross Strand, January 2024. Images: Angela Kelly (WildAtlanticimageaok)

Boundaries

Watcher: She's gone. She's been spotted in *Sligo*.

Mariner: Ok, let's go.

Watcher: No. It has to be Mayo.

Mariner: But the whale isn't in Mayo anymore.

Watcher: Then I'll wait until she comes back.

Mariner: And if she doesn't?

Watcher:

Mariner: The whales don't care about county lines. It's all their sea.

Watcher: And there's a boat.

Watcher as wave rider

Feet lifting from the slick of the deck, I braid my arms to the barrier at the back.

'The stern,' Mariner reminds me, and I glare across mist to say 'do I look like I give a shit?'

'We have a fair idea where to find them,' said the fisherman turned whale guide, but this choppiness has come in sudden. 'Hmm, never this quiet,' he says.

All life seems to flee.

Two piss-taking dolphins, quick slips of slate. Puffins run across the water like windup toys.

I lose my footing, grip tighter. This tin bucket holds my life. A wave curls over us, soaking the deck. Is this risk? I imagine my child at home, orphaned over my ridiculous pursuits.

Is it any wonder that man launched such an attack on the ocean and its contents? Who could ever have imagined that *we*, tiny people, could defeat *this*. Yet (all together!) we *have* depleted and destroyed the sea: stripped its bed of life, clogged its guts with plastic, bleached its coral, made its orcas barren, turned the boiler up. How powerful we humans are. Not that any of this would stop an errant wave drowning our boat and its naïve passengers.

The photographers, raingear pulled sphincter-tight around their readied faces, return cameras to bags. Disappointment swells. I want to cry. The water is bucking us off. Nothing to be done. The jobs lost, deals not struck, the life that wouldn't stick, all my good intentions, my obsessions, fucked away. The clouds break. The boat turns. All around is a turmoil of grey.

A little more about the whales
(as we know now)

Irish waters are currently home to approximately 26 different kinds of cetaceans. Some of these are considered vagrants, coming into Irish waters in unusual circumstances. But many, such as the humpback, blue whale, fin whale, and sperm whale, are annual habitants of our waters.

Humpback whales are rorquals, the largest group of baleen whales. The adult size ranges from 46-56 feet and weighs up to 40 tonnes. They are known for their breaching, their songs, and the distinctive arch their back makes when sounding, which gives them their name. In the late 19th century, early 20th century, their global numbers were approximately 231,700. Their numbers fell to 5000 in the 1960s. Their numbers currently stand at approximately 135,000.

Ireland has a regular humpback population, with 126 individuals included in the Irish Humpback whale photo ID Catalogue.

Blue whales are the largest known animal ever to have existed. Adults reach approximately 98 feet and weigh 199 tonnes. In the late 19th century, early 20th century, their global numbers were approximately 340,280. As of 2018, the numbers were estimated to be between 10,000 and 25,000.

They are migratory and can be found in the deep waters of the continental shelf during the summer and autumn months.

Fin whales are also known as the common rorqual. They're the second-longest cetacean. They grow up to 85 feet and 88 tonnes. In the late 19th century, early 20th century, their global numbers were 762,400. It is estimated their numbers are currently close to 100,000. Fin whales are still hunted in Iceland and Japan.

There have been over 60 individuals identified in Irish waters, many returning each year. They can be spotted along the south coast, but like the humpbacks, are moving north.

Sei whales are the third largest rorqual. They grow up to 64 feet and 28 tonnes. In the late 19th century, early 20th century, their global numbers were approximately 392,300. Their numbers are estimated to be between 57,000 and 65,000.

There is little known about their numbers in Irish waters, with only five sightings in recent years.

Sperm whales are the largest species of tooth whale and the world's largest toothed predator. They grow up to 59 feet and 42 tonnes. There were approximately 2 million sperm whales in the world before whaling escalated in the 18th century. Their numbers are now around 850,000.

In Ireland, they occur in offshore deep waters along the continental shelf.

North Atlantic right whales are a baleen whale amongst the most endangered whales in the world. In the late 19th century, early 20th century, their global numbers were 84,100.

Since IWDG records began in 1990 there had been no sightings of North Atlantic right whales in Irish waters. That is until 15 July 2024, when a single North Atlantic right whale was spotted in the waters of Donegal Bay.[51]

TWO FILMS

We meet again, Norway

I watch a documentary about modern Norwegian whaling. Norway rejected the IWC's moratorium and continues the hunting of minke whales to this day. Sighting surveys show the minke population to be stable at in or around a hundred thousand.

The whalers talk of the thrill. Of getting a taste for the hunt. It is *exciting*. One man has left a career in the oil industry to become a whaler.

They haul a whale onto the deck. Footage shows the slitting of her underbelly, and the release of a small but perfectly formed whale from within. This, in case the viewer needs reminding, is not a fish.

The animal is stripped of its blubber and meat. The blubber is white. It sits atop the meat like icing on a slice of red velvet cake. The skeleton is shoved overboard. Bulbous sacks of pink float to the surface.

This isn't historical. This is now. But this aspect doesn't surprise me as it should. Butchery as industry has not ceased. Perhaps the question should be, why do we balk at the inhumanity of killing whales, but not at the beef industry, not at the rampant wars, famine, genocide that happen not in the past, but far away?

Killer, whale

I'm watching another documentary, *Keiko: the untold story of the star of Free Willy*.

I, like many children in the nineties, loved *Free Willy*, the story of an orca's return to the wild. I was unaware that its star, Keiko, was not free until a charity project funded by fans of the film resulted in him being freed in 2002. He was carefully monitored during his reintroduction to the ocean to keep him safe, and Keiko swam independently from Iceland to Norway, arriving in Norway in good physical condition. But Keiko did not assimilate with any wild pod. Orcas have families not unlike humans, and he eventually returned to shore for human contact. The charity set up support for him with his caretakers living close by. He died in 2003.

One interview subject in the documentary is Naomi Rose, PhD, a senior scientist at Humane Society International. Of her observations in the film, one struck me in particular:

'It's a full-time job being an orca. It's a full-time job being a predator. I know that some of the public display facilities…consider it a benefit of captivity that they take away this burden from them, this constant need of having to look for food. But it's the way they make a living. It's their job. When you take that away from them a huge part of their identity is removed. A huge part of their daily activity and challenge is taken away from them. A great deal of their ability to make choices and decisions is taken away.'

Some of the interview subjects, especially those who took direct care of Keiko, could be accused of anthropomorphising him, assuming loneliness, relief, humour.

But we can't assume that cetaceans don't feel. Many studies have indicated that animals experience emotion. We know orcas are highly intelligent. Scientists have found that whales live in families, experience culture, and possibly have language. The concept of anthropomorphising is dependent on human attributes belonging only to humans.

When I think of how much knowledge about cetaceans has come on in the centuries since whaling began, I consider it likely that there is at least that much that we still do not know about them.

If anthropomorphising is a risk, the worst-case scenario is misplaced empathy. But without empathy, we get slaughter.

It's an easy tactic. Make your prey into an opponent. Use language to warp the subject, until the language feels like fact.

Beast   *sea monster*   *devil of the deep*

Barbarous   *savage*   *infidel*

Intelligence

In *How to Speak Whale: a voyage into the future of animal communication*, Tom Mustill looks at how advancing technology could increase our understanding of, and empathy with, cetaceans. By recording whale sounds on a huge scale, scientists have discovered patterns and variations that show us whale song is more than just noise. Cetaceans communicate vocally. Populations of whales that don't interact, for example the humpbacks of the northern and southern hemispheres, speak with different vocabularies: their songs are completely different.[52]

Non-profit organisation Project CETI, founded by biologist David Gruber, is working to design AI tools which will allow humans to communicate with sperm whales. By recording millions of whale codas alongside analysing behaviour of the animals, there is hope that they may find the meaning behind the sequence of clicks made by sperm whales. That is, if there is complex meaning. Linguists argue that even complex animal vocalising does not have the communications systems needed to be defined as language.

In 2023, the project discovered previously unknown dimensions of sperm whale vocalisation that are 'analogous to human vowels and diphthongs'.[53] By 2024, the project had learned of an entire phonetic alphabet.

'Sperm whales communicate primarily using sequences of short bursts of clicks with varying inter-click intervals, known as codas. The paper reports previously undescribed variations in coda structure that are sensitive to the conversational context in which they occur. This study shows that coda types are not arbitrary, but rather that they form a newly discovered combinatorial coding system in which the musical concepts of rubato and ornamentation combine with two categorical, context-independent features known as rhythm and tempo, by analogy to musical terminology. Rhythm, tempo, rubato and ornamentation can be freely combined. This gives rise to a large inventory of distinguishable codas — a "sperm whale phonetic alphabet" that makes it possible to systematically explain observed variability in coda structure.

"This discovery marks a profound moment in advancing our understanding of sperm whales," said Dr. Gruber, "It opens up the possibility that sperm whales have an incredibly complex and nuanced communication system – and inspires us to continue on our whale listening journey."[54]

It is a small but significant step towards understanding what, if anything, sperm whales are saying. Whales may well have language after all, and there's a chance that humans have the technology that will prove it, as long as they have the time, funding, and living whales, to do so.

A world of Ahabs

What Dr Rose said in the documentary keeps coming back to me. The daily survival of a wild animal. It is the drive that occupies them, challenges them, keeps the circle of living things turning.

Is it the *somewhere* in the brain that hasn't evolved to catch up with supermarkets and IVF that keeps us needing?

While the monomaniacal antihero of Melville's novel may be at the extreme end of the scale, there is a reason the character is so well remembered.

Desire. The injustice of not getting what you want. The injustice of life at all. Crazed pursuit. I have felt it, all the fury and impotence of an outraged toddler.

I may be guilty now of zoomorphism. Assigning a purely biological drive to human behaviour. But I know what it is to be an animal. To bleed, to feel pain, to lust. I have seen the glint of a man's eye that marks me as prey. I have felt fury strong enough I tasted blood.

Yet, I have wallowed in the emptiness of days, struck by the pointlessness of it all. Fantasised (foolish, selfish girl) that if I worked the fields like long ago, I wouldn't have time for all this *angst*. Everyone needs work, a purpose. I spear my poems like fish. Just give me something to pursue.

Here I am, like so many before me, taking to the sea to chase the whales.

Hunter

Unlike the whalers I read about, I am a woman. I tell myself my obsession does not equate with Ahab's bloodlust.

In school we learned about early people. Pre-agricultural and pre-industrial societies survived through hunting and gathering.

The men would hunt.

The women gathered.

If we stick with this biological essentialism, hunting is a male activity. Maybe the reasons behind this were physical strength, child-minding, or an inherently masculine need to seek and destroy. That hunter drive: to seek, to consume. Is that the drive that sent men over oceans, on to new lands to claim as their own? Is it what pulled whales from the water, oil from the ground? The space race, uncountable wars, the extinction of species, a patriarchal system that has driven the earth to its limit?

Men live with the expectation of being a hunter. The belief that it is in men's nature to hunt, to be violent, has driven and excused centuries of destructive male behaviour. Could a societal restructuring towards the gathering end of the gender binary save us? The nurturing female vs the hunting male. Gathering fruit, vegetables. Gathering our children to us. It would make a tidy metaphor.

I don't put much weight in speculation.

Comparisons are made with the reproductive urge, the male of the species seeking out the female to mate, yet research shows the multiple factors at play in human sex drive, including social influences. At a time in science when such binaries are being questioned, the verdict is very much still out. More recent studies suggest women hunted too, and still do in modern hunter-gatherer societies. Our concept of ancient gender roles is incorrect, informed partially by bias in the original science.

That whalers were exclusively men has more to do with the complex gender politics of modern societies than a biological urge to kill. It is human nature to pursue. It is human nature, as it is the nature of all living things, to survive.

When pursuit and survival contradict each other, what then?

SAVE THE WHALE
(save the world)

Recovery

The link[55] lands in my inbox like a toll.

> For the 40 years after the end of commercial whaling in 1976,
> humpback whale populations in the North Pacific Ocean
> exhibited a prolonged period of recovery. Using mark–recapture
> methods on the largest individual photo-identification dataset
> ever assembled for a cetacean, we estimated annual ocean-basin-
> wide abundance for the species from 2002 through 2021. Trends
> in annual estimates describe strong post-whaling era population
> recovery from 16 875 (± 5955) in 2002 to a peak abundance
> estimate of 33 488 (± 4455) in 2012. An apparent 20 percent
> decline from 2012 to 2021, 33 488 (± 4455) to 26 662 (± 4192),
> suggests the population abruptly reached carrying capacity due to
> loss of prey resources. This was particularly evident for humpback
> whales wintering in Hawai'i, where, by 2021, estimated abundance
> had declined by 34 percent from a peak in 2013, down to
> abundance levels previously seen in 2006, and contrasted to an
> absence of decline in Mainland Mexico breeding humpbacks. The
> strongest marine heatwave recorded globally to date during the
> 2014–2016 period appeared to have altered the course of species
> recovery, with enduring effects.

All is not saved.

> The end of the industrial whaling era left oceans largely empty of
> great whales. Yet with no species hunted to global extinction
> during this period, full recovery became a possibility. For
> humpback whales, steady population growth was the 40-year
> trend in the North Pacific, and it is to be celebrated that
> humpback whales appeared sufficiently recovered to qualify for
> partial delisting from legal protected status regimes in the USA
> and Canada. Ironically, the timing of legal conservation status
> changes for the species was coincident with the dramatic ocean-
> warming-induced decline documented in this study. Some
> populations of humpback whales may no longer be a priority for
> endangered species conservation funding, but now offer high value

as an indicator species of ocean-basin-wide ecosystem health in a world where we can expect increased frequency and severity of marine heatwaves.

All is not lost.

Threats

Though whaling has been stopped in most of the world, there are numerous threats to cetaceans.

- Habitat loss caused by development of offshore infrastructure, bottom trawling, and ocean warming.

- Contaminants such as polychlorinated biphenyls negatively impact reproduction in cetaceans and are believed to be responsible for the functional extinction of Scottish orcas.

- Plastic is being found in the digestive tracts of cetaceans, as well as microplastics being embedded in their bodies.

- Noise pollution from sonar, seismic surveys, shipping, drilling, military sonar. For creatures that depend on acoustics to survive, this pollution can lead to habitat loss, stress, and long-term physical issues.

- Entanglement in fishing equipment is a major cause of mortality in whales.

- Bycatch is estimated to be responsible for 300,000 cetacean deaths each year.

- Overfishing removes the cetaceans' prey from their habitat, leaving them with insufficient food to survive.

- Increased marine traffic in recent decades means that ship strikes, a collision between a vessel and a whale are causing more fatalities. It's estimated that 20,000 whales are killed by ship strikes each year.

- Commercial whaling is ongoing in Iceland, Norway, and Japan.

What have the whales ever done for us?

If you put inherent value on sentient life, then the extinction of any animal is a tragedy in itself. Not everyone does, reserving such value for humans only. Regardless, what we forget is that if the whales die, we die with them.

Whale and Dolphin Conservation (WDC) is a global charity that works to protect cetaceans. They describe their work as being 'to transform our view of the ocean and the extraordinary life it contains – from a "sustainable resource" to be managed and extracted from, to a living system: an insurance policy against our own extinction.'[56]

Whales are invaluable in the fight against climate change. They are massive carbon sinks. Quite literally, they absorb huge amounts of carbon and when they die, they sink to the ocean floor, bringing that carbon with them. While some whale carcasses are consumed more quickly at lower depths, when they fall into the abyssal zone, coming to rest at a depth of more than 1000 metres, they become what is known as a whale fall. In addition to trapping carbon on the ocean floor, a whale fall provides an ecosystem for hundreds of deep sea creatures for up to 50 years.

The nutrient-rich faeces and urine whales release near the surface fuel the growth of phytoplankton, microscopic ocean creatures which capture approximately 40 percent of all CO_2 produced and produce at least 50 percent of the oxygen in the atmosphere.

Whales are migratory creatures. While it's difficult to protect them without international cooperation, each country can contribute by protecting habitats and increasing political pressure to make these protections global. In Ireland, environmental NGOs have come together to form Fair Seas, a coalition calling for 30 percent of Ireland's ocean territory to be fully protected by 2030. Their aim is to see Ireland 'become a world leader in marine protection, giving our species, habitats and coastal communities the opportunity to thrive.'[57]

When the whaling companies came to Ireland in the early 20th century, there was no legislation in place to govern whaling. Legislation created by Ray Burke gave fossil fuel companies the most favourable terms in the world, to the detriment of the country and the environment. To avoid exploitation, the laws need to be in place. Legislation on Marine Protected Areas (the MPA Act) will be the first time Ireland has had legislation dedicated to protecting our marine environment. The Act will fall under the 30 by 30 EU Biodiversity Strategy which aims to protect a minimum of 30 percent of all European waters by 2030.

Energy

The IWDG continued to fight in the cetaceans' corner as the Corrib gas controversy unfolded. They made a submission to the Corrib Gas Environmental Impact Assessment Scoping document in 2001. When the results of this assessment failed to address their submission, they brought it to the Department of Marine, Enterprise Oil and the National Parks and Wildlife Service. Eventually, they pursued it to the European Court of Justice, which resulted in a judgment against Ireland in 2007.

In a statement that year, the IWDG said:

'At present most of the issues the IWDG raised have been addressed and we feel confident that direct impacts on cetaceans in the area will be minimal. Indirect impacts through degradation of water quality, food supply etc are very hard to quantify and assess and will require detailed studies. There have been a number of detailed studies on marine mammals in Broadhaven Bay, carried out by CMRC [Coastal and Marine Resources Centre] at UCC. These studies were funded by Enterprise Energy Ireland Ltd.'[58]

drill gas ... Inishkea West field ... full support for the gas project

members of the ...

There is all sorts of stuff you need to find out for yourselves

sceptical

déjà vu all over again

gas will provide ... guarantees

economic argument ... flies in the face of current government policy.

to support the gas coming ashore from the new field.

take climate change seriously   still a place for gas exploration.

a stop gap

other technologies

Commerce   investment

bring people into north Mayo   solar panels

support this project

The climate crisis is impacting the cetaceans. Changes in distribution and movement, reproduction, and feed locations are already happening.

To limit the effects of the climate crisis, we must stop extracting fossil fuels. Yet, deep sea mining for minerals necessary in some green technology disrupts the whales' habitat in myriad ways.

It is not conservation which drives the mining. The industry is worth trillions. But we have seen that green technology is unlikely to replace fossil fuels without social pressure and the systemic suppression of the industry. The problem won't be part of the solution. The frustration can seem insurmountable when even supposed green energy has negative environmental effects. How can society move in a direction that limits negative effects and prioritises the right to life?

I spoke to the CEO of the IWDG, Dr Simon Berrow, in April 2024. When I asked him about the Corrib gas controversy, he said that more than 20 years on, there is no evidence of long-term negative impact on cetaceans in this specific case.

The direct potential damage to the cetaceans from the Corrib gas extraction was mitigated by the work of the IWDG. However, it is not just the local impact of such projects which must be considered, but the effect of more fossil fuels on a rapidly warming climate.

Berrow noted that by working with industries and government agencies, more can be learned about cetaceans and how to protect them:

> Offshore windfarms and other such industries, their impacts can be mitigated. They can become more positive by making them, for example, bottom trawler exclusion areas. Biodiversity enhancing measures should have to be included alongside windfarms and other offshore developments. We need a good scientific baseline to find which measures improve their food sources.

We can't return to a pre-industrial world. We must work with what is here.

To wake is to watch

As I read and reread, the lines begin to blur. Dr Berrow speaks about the valuable data that comes from the surveys paid for by oil companies. Burfield's report of the Belmullet whaling station was for the British Association of the Advancement of Science. It provided information on the cetaceans that have since been used to establish a baseline for whale populations in Irish waters.

Every doctor learns his trade at the table of the dead.

I write in the language my ancestors feared.

We are made of the things that broke us.

I've been thinking about the Irish tradition of waking the dead. Keeping watch over the body in the home. The Inishkea station workers would take three days off work for a wake.

It is widely thought the wake has origins in pre-Christian times, the jovial atmosphere rooted in a celebration of the life lived and the life to come in the next world.

An American wake is a wake for someone still living who's about to emigrate. Ireland famously lost as many to emigration as death during the famine, and it didn't stop in the 20th century. So many left Irish shores, unlikely to return. As with heaven, they may have gone off to have a better life in a new world, but that didn't erase the grief of those left behind. Emigration hasn't stopped, though Skype and transatlantic flights ease the permanence.

One theory about wakes, tracing back centuries, is that the body was kept watch over to be sure the person was really dead. This has led to the misconception that the term 'wake' was to do with waiting in case the dead would 'wake up'. It means to remain awake and hold a vigil. Linguistically, its origins are in Germanic and Old English. The Dutch *waken* is connected to the German *wachen*.

To wake is to watch.

"No one will protect what they don't care about;
and no one will care about what they have never experienced."

– David Attenborough

Watching the horizon for a returning ship. Watching your own hands clasped in prayer for a reunion after death. Watching what we can't control, what has slipped from our grasp. To celebrate, to honour, to wish it wasn't happening.

That's what it can feel like, loving the natural world in a time like this.

≈

Dr Berrow talks about both the risks and potential around whale watching.

> We are becoming a nation of nature watchers, becoming more interested. But we have to do it responsibly, through education and positive feedback. For example, if a boat is bringing people out to see humpbacks in Donegal Bay, that might be the only year they do it because we don't know if the whales will come back, but if we know more about the whales, we can protect their food sources. If marine tourism is viable, it gives the incentive to invest in doing things safely and properly.

Do my noble intentions justify my ruthless pursuit? I suspect my intentions are not as pure as I tell myself they are.

LÁN MARA

Not much fishing off Rusheen now,
mainly lobsters skinny in their pots.

While supertrawlers dredge the trough,
our boatmen bring tourists out

to this island where you glimpse
the past while snorkelling in turquoise
shallows, plummeting fathoms
and deep-sea of so many wayfarers
no shanty will rhyme or remember.

Out of history we heave, out of heritage we climb,
But all things must sink or swim in their time.

All around us, a residue of the hunted –
long-finished dregs of labour choking
the air, the economy's dearth,
no ledger book for the misty mornings,
men numb from butchery, mammals
curves, like marble hacked into elegance.

    Out of history we heave, out of heritage we climb,
    But all things must sink or swim in their time.

The cove once soupy as kerosene at this Babel
of stench and scale, the mainland din
of the dances. Children's voices
reciting *Ár nAthair atá ar neamh*
from the school echo in rhythm
to the breakers as the bell for quitting time
is rung for all across this isle.

    Out of history we heave, out of heritage we climb,
    But all things must sink or swim in their time.

The barometer declines
muted warning of the swells rabid
and whirling off the peninsula,
candles no longer flickering
in the glassless frames
for the men of '27 who didn't come ashore.
No rosaries clutched, no sign of a homecoming.

  Out of history we heave, out of heritage we climb,
  But all things must sink or swim in their time.

Caithfidh an fharraige a cuid fhéin a fháil:
The sea must get its own share.
Guilt expunged on the tráigha.
Lán Mara coming for our island and yours.

  Out of history we heave, out of heritage we climb,
  But all things must sink or swim in their time.

Waves are called to worship by the shore.
We get reacquainted with the classics
on audiobook, pore over exquisitely-
reproduced engravings of the stranded
beasts with cavernous jaws, play recordings
of their sunken psalmody on a loop.
Wonder how an island people ignore
our vast western waters?

  Out of history we heave, out of heritage we climb,
  But all things must sink or swim in their time.

Watcher as whaler

Again. I will try again. A text: 5pm Tuesday. The summer's almost over, soon the boat will have returned to fishing, and the whales will move on. I have to see them, to finish this, to let go.

We drive to the pier. At 16:45, with no sign of the boat, I call.

'We're coming back in, out all day, we'd given up, but...'

Oh, that *but*.

The sea is calmer today. Children flop from paddle boards, seal pups, sandy-handed and salt haired. The zip on my coat has jammed with rust.

The boat moves easily through the water. Rise and fall. All the birds fly with us towards the sharp white line of the horizon. We've been told to watch for the birds. Diving. A swarm of them like crows above carrion. They are whale diviners.

I ask about that. Apparently, they can be caught like flies in a snapdragon. Dead birds floating near a feeding frenzy is not uncommon. Collateral damage. Guess they figure it's worth the risk.

'A blow! A blow!'

The water stills to a plastic smoothness. Rings of aquamarine. Kittwakes frantic above.

It's so quiet. Their breath comes in recognisable spurts. Their mouths, because there are *two*, Queen Medb and her companion, swallow the ocean whole.

I am blank.

I wait for the rush of relief, of awe, of joy. I can feel my face grinning, but my lust has not been satisfied.

I want to dive into the water, swim beside them. Yet I know that that would only spur another urge, to touch their fins, to wish to move like them. That childish urge to transform into something else.

Cameras shutter. Seven small rectangles capture the scenes.

Shoot shoot shoot.

Capture.

'Did you get it?' I ask Mariner. He is gazing at the scene, mouth slightly open.

My shitty phone.

'I should have brought a camera,' I mutter half to him and half to myself.

No.

It's never enough. Capturing an image is not capturing the thing. Am I *trying* to capture it? This rush of the hunt that I've been chasing won't get me anywhere.

It's never enough.

When faced with such enormity. When reminded of our otherness. That we are one variation of a myriad life. That blood and milk flow through breathing creatures so far from us that we could never hope to understand. This urge to understand, to conquer, to control.

Even if I got the perfect photograph. Even if I were in the water astride the animal. Even if I had harpooned and hauled it aboard myself. It would never be enough. There is a barrier I can't cross. There will be no letting go.

So, I put the phone away, and I watch.

Black and barnacled. Throats swelling with water. Filtering food. Like every nature documentary I have seen, except, not. The incomparable texture of the viewing.

The hump, sheen of rain on tarmac. The smell, kelpy but undeniably mammalian.

We follow, a distance kept. And then, behind the boat, one throws his tail to us. Dolphins fling themselves from the water, as if to emphasise their relative slightness.

Then,

quick as something that has already happened,

even as it is happening,

an eruption of water breaking,

her whole body breaches.

My face is sprayed by the crash and slap of blubber on surface. The sea crackles white where she has already vanished. Our collective gasp ripples in a mirror to those watery reverberations. My eyes are lined with the image of her enormous belly.

We see another flick, her companion beside the boat with his bristly smile. But soon, they are moving on. To follow them, how far would we follow? The light gets shorter each evening as the summer fades. I don't get to make the call.

To save is to know, not own. Not to witness, but to watch.

As the boat recedes, I keep watch.

Watch the waves, forget the waiting, it's the watching.

Senses attuned, the rush and satisfaction of capture (image, moment). Forget it.

Know they might rise again, or that may have been your final glimpse.

Watch.

That's the thing about a wake. You suspect you won't see them again, but you can't be sure.

Humpback in Broadhaven Bay, 2023. Image: Brendan Quinn

Humpback in Broadhaven Bay, 2023. Image: Brendan Quinn

Humpback in Broadhaven Bay, 2023. Image: Brendan Quinn

Humpback in Broadhaven Bay, 2023. Image: Brendan Quinn

Humpback in Donegal Bay. Image: Gary Burrows

Humpback in Donegal Bay. Image: Gary Burrows

Humpback in Donegal Bay. Image: Gary Burrows

Humpback in Broadhaven Bay. Image: Brendan Quinn

References

1   C. Ryan, 'Insights into the biology and ecology of whales in Ireland 100 years ago from archived whaling data', *Irish Naturalists' Journal*, 39 (2022), 24–35.

2   Annals of Ulster, https://www.celt.dias.ie/publications/online/vikings-temporarily-removed/data.html, accessed 14 July 2024.

3   Common descriptions of cetaceans in whaling era texts.

4   Commissioners for Publishing the Ancient Laws and Institutes of Ireland, *Ancient Laws and Institutes of Ireland*, Volume 1 (Dublin, 1865: Printed for H.M. Stationery Office; A. Thom). (https://archive.org/search.php?query=creator%3A%22Ireland.+Commissioners+for+Publishing+the+Ancient+Laws+and+Institutes+of+Ireland%22, accessed 12 July 2024)

5   Arthur E.J. Went, 'Whaling from Ireland', *The Journal of the Royal Society of Antiquaries of Ireland*, 98: 1 (1968), 31–36. JSTOR, http://www.jstor.org/stable/25509669, accessed 13 March 2024.

6   James Paterson, *A Treatise on the Fishery Laws of the United Kingdom: Including the Laws of Angling* (London, 1863: Macmillan).

7   R.W.A. McNeary, 'Eighteenth century whaling and shark fishery at Inver, Donegal Bay', *Donegal Annual*, 60 (2008), 82-98.

8   James McParlan, *Statistical Survey of the County of Donegal* (1802: Graisberry and Campbell).

9   James Fairley, *Irish Whales and Whaling* (Belfast, 1981: Blackstaff).

10   A sample of descriptions of the Irish people from historical sources ranging from 1188-1945.

11   Alexander Shand quoted in Rita Nolan, *Within the Mullet* (1998: Standard Printers).

12   Rita Nolan, *Within the Mullet* (1998: Standard Printers).

13   James Fairley, *Irish Whales and Whaling* (Belfast, 1981: Blackstaff).

14   William Shakespeare, *The Merchant of Venice* (1598).

15   C. Ryan, 'Insights into the biology and ecology of whales in Ireland 100 years ago from archived whaling data', *Irish Naturalists' Journal*, 39 (2022), 24–35.

16   Ibid.

17   *Connacht Telegraph*, 7 December 1912.

18   'Völuspá', *The Poetic Edda (Poems of the Vikings: The Elder Edda)*, trans. Patricia Terry (1990: University of Pennsylvania Press).

19   James Fairley, *Irish Whales and Whaling* (Belfast, 1981: Blackstaff).

20   Paul Henry, as quoted in James Fairley, *Irish Whales and Whaling* (Belfast, 1981: Blackstaff)

21   Rita Nolan, *Within the Mullet* (1998: Standard Printers).

22 Typescript transcripts of tape recorded interviews by Dr J.S. Fairley, Zoology Department, University College, Galway, with persons associated with the Arranmore and Blacksod whaling companies. They were prepared as part of Dr Fairley's research for his book, *Irish Whales and Whaling* (Belfast, 1981: Blackstaff), 1977–1978, courtesy of the Public Record Office of Northern Ireland.

23 Ibid.

24 Ibid.

25 Ibid.

26 Ibid.

27 Ibid.

28 Ibid.

29 Ibid.

30 S.T. Burfield, 'Belmullet whaling station report of the eightieth meeting of the British association for the advancement of science Portsmouth' (1911), 121–25.

31 Typescript transcripts of tape recorded interviews by Dr J.S. Fairley, Zoology Department, University College, Galway, with persons associated with the Arranmore and Blacksod whaling companies. They were prepared as part of Dr Fairley's research for his book, *Irish Whales and Whaling* (Belfast, 1981: Blackstaff), 1977–1978, courtesy of the Public Record Office of Northern Ireland.

32 Ibid.

33 Ibid and Rita Nolan, *Within the Mullet* (1998: Standard Printers).

34 Rita Nolan, *Within the Mullet* (1998: Standard Printers).

35 Letter from chairman of Mayo County Council to Fisheries Branch of the Department, *The Freeman's Journal*, 6 December 1909.

36 Typescript transcripts of tape recorded interviews by Dr J.S. Fairley, Zoology Department, University College, Galway, with persons associated with the Arranmore and Blacksod whaling companies. They were prepared as part of Dr Fairley's research for his book, *Irish Whales and Whaling* (Belfast, 1981: Blackstaff), 1977–1978, courtesy of the Public Record Office of Northern Ireland.

37 Arthur E.J. Went, 'Whaling from Ireland', *The Journal of the Royal Society of Antiquaries of Ireland*, 98: 1 (1968), 31–36.
    JSTOR, http://www.jstor.org/stable/25509669, accessed 13 March 2024.

38 *Irish Press*, 4 March 1933, accessed via Mayo County Libraries.

39 S.T. Burfield, 'Belmullet whaling station report of the eightieth meeting of the British association for the advancement of science Portsmouth' (1911), 121–25.

40 R. York, 'Why Petroleum Did Not Save the Whales', *Socius*, 3 (2017).

41 Ibid.

42 Ibid.

43 Ibid.

44 'Ireland – A Sanctuary for Whales and Dolphins: A Discussion Document', produced by the Irish Whale and Dolphin Group (1993).

45 Lorna Siggins, *Once Upon A Time in the West: the Corrib Gas Controversy* (Ireland, 2010: Transworld).

46 Richard Ellis, *Men and Whales* (New York, 1991: Knopf).

47 https://www.cshwhalingmuseum.org/blog/a-woman-has-an-awful-lot-to-thank-a-whale-for, accessed 13 July 2024.

48 James Fairley, *Irish Whales and Whaling* (Belfast, 1981: Blackstaff).

49 IWDG Newsletter, April 1992.

50 https://iwdg.ie/mayo-whale-and-dolphin-survey/, accessed 13 July 2024.

51 https://iwdg.ie/1st-irish-record-of-a-north-atlantic-right-whale-validated-by-iwdg

52 https://www.royalholloway.ac.uk/about-us/news/new-research-reveals-why-whale-song-culture-differs-between-northern-and-southern-hemispheres/, accessed 13 July 2024.

53 Gasper Begus, Ronald Sprouse, Andrej Leban, Miles Silva, and Shane Gero, 'Vowels and Diphthongs in Sperm Whales' (December 2023). https://doi.org/10.31219/osf.io/285cs, accessed 13 July 2024.

54 https://www.projectceti.org/blog-posts/sperm-whale-phonetic-alphabet-proposed-for-the-first-time, accessed 13 July 2024.

55 https://royalsocietypublishing.org/doi/10.1098/rsos.231462#, accessed 13 July 2024.

56 https://uk.whales.org/2021/10/26/save-the-whale-save-the-world-because-our-lives-depend-on-it/, accessed 13 July 2024.

57 https://fairseas.ie/about/, accessed 13 July 2024.

58 https://iwdg.ie/iwdg-respond-to-criticism-over-corrib-gas/, accessed 13 July 2024.

Image list

p. 91:	Burfield, S.T. (1912), Belmullet whaling station - report to the committee. Report of the eightieth meeting of the British association for the advancement of science Portsmouth: 1911, 121–25.
p. 93:	A 70-foot fin whale, plate 14 from the series Whaling Fishing/The Blacksod Bay, Whaling Co. Ltd., 1911. 86.139.002.014* Worswick, Collection of the Herbert F. Johnson Museum of Art, Cornell University, Image courtesy of the Johnson Museum
p. 94:	Ibid. The first cut, plate 24 from the series Whaling Fishing/The Blacksod Bay Whaling Co. Ltd., 1911. 86.139.002.024*
pp 95–6:	Burfield, S.T. (1912), Belmullet whaling station - report to the committee. Report of the eightieth meeting of the British association for the advancement of science Portsmouth:1911, 121–25.
p. 97:	Image by Jack Leonard. Courtesy of Anthony Leonard
p. 98:	Carcase [carcass] consisting of the entrails, plate 39 from the series Whaling Fishing/The Blacksod Bay Whaling Co. Ltd., 1911. 86.139.002.039* Worswick, Collection of the Herbert F. Johnson Museum of Art, Cornell University. Image courtesy of the Johnson Museum
p. 98:	Burfield, S.T. (1912), Belmullet whaling station - report to the committee. Report of the eightieth meeting of the British association for the advancement of science Portsmouth: 1911, 121–25.
p. 99:	Whale on the dock, from Whaling album, 1911. 86.139.017.002* Worswick,Collection of the Herbert F. Johnson Museum of Art, Cornell University, Image courtesy of the Johnson Museum
p. 100:	Reproductions by Paul Kinsella. Images courtesy of Patrick Geraghty. Photographer unknown
p. 101:	Image by Paul Kinsella (2024)
p. 102:	Reproductions by Paul Kinsella. Images courtesy of Patrick Geraghty. Photographer unknown
p. 105:	*Irish Press*, 1933. Accessed via Mayo County Library
p. 110:	Image by Paul Kinsella (2024)
p. 113:	Irish Whale and Dolphin Group newsletter, September 1991, courtesy of Simon Berrow and the Irish Whale and Dolphin Group
p. 120:	Image by Paul Kinsella (2023)
p. 138:	Humpback tail with footprint, Alice Kinsella, 2023
pp 142–3:	Irish Whale and Dolphin Group newsletter, April 1992, courtesy of Simon Berrow and the Irish Whale and Dolphin Group
p. 147:	Map by Éadaoin Ní Néill
p. 149:	Acoustic and visual survey of cetaceans off the Mullet Peninsula, Co. Mayo, *Irish Naturalists' Journal,* Volume 26, 1999
p. 154:	Irish Whale and Dolphin Group at work, Fin whale, Ross Strand, January 2024. Images by WildAtlanticimageaok, courtesy of Angela Kelly

p. 169:   https://www.mayonews.ie/news/home/1301074/spc-members-urged-to-inform-themselves-on-gas-exploration-off-mayo-coast.html

pp 179–82:   Images by Brendan Quinn

pp 183–5:   Images by Gary Burrows

p. 186:   Image by Brendan Quinn

Bibliography

Coleridge, Samuel Taylor, *The Rhyme of the Ancient Mariner* (1798).

Dornan, Brian, *Mayo's Lost Islands* (2000: Four Courts Press)

Doyle, Arthur Conan, *Dangerous Work: Diary of an Arctic Explorer* (2012: British Library)

Ellis, Richard, *Men and Whales* (New York, 1991: Knopf).

Fairley, James, *Irish Whales and Whaling* (Belfast, 1981: Blackstaff).

Flavel, John, *Navigation Spiritualised* (1797).

Gibson, Gregory, *Demon of the Waters* (2002: Backbay Books).

Henry, Françoisem *The Inishkea Journals* (2012: Four Courts Press).

Hoare, Philip, *Leviathan, or The Whale* (2008: Fourth Estate).

Joyce, Patrick W. (trans.), *Immram Maele Dúin (The Voyage of Máel Dúin)* (1879).

Mair, Alexander William (trans.), *The Halieutica - Oppian* (1922: Loeb Classical Library).

Marsden, Philip, *Summer Isles: A Voyage of Imagination* (2019).

McNeary, R.W.A., 'Guns, harpoons, lances, casks and every [necessary] article: An account of the history and archaeology of an eighteenth-century shore-based whaling and basking shark fishery in Donegal Bay', *Historical Archaeology*, 41(3), 115-124 (2007).

Melville, Herman, *Moby-Dick* (1851).

Murphy, Richard, *Sailing to an Island* (1963: Faber & Faber).

Mustill, Tom, *How to Speak Whale* (2022: William Collins).

Nolan, Rita, *Within the Mullet* (1998: Standard Printers).

Nowak, Mark, *Coal Mountain Elementary* (2009: Coffee House Press).

O'Boyle, Sean, *The Irish Song Tradition* (1976: Gilbert Dalton).

O'Donoghue, Denis (trans.), *Navigatio Sancti Brendani Abbatis (Voyage of Saint Brendan the Abbot)*, (1893).

O'Raghallaigh, Tomás Bán, *I gCeart Lar Mo Dhaoine – Amongst Our Own, The Inniskeas* (2017).

Philbrick, Nathaniel, *In the Heart of the Sea* (2000: Viking Press).

Robertson, Robert B., *Of Whales and Men* (1954: Knopf).

Rukeyser, Muriel, *Western Book of the Dead* (2018).

Sanderson, Ivan T., *Follow the Whale* (New York, 1956: Bramhal House).

Siggins, Lorna, *Once Upon A Time in the West: the Corrib Gas Controversy* (Ireland, 2010: Transworld).

Terry, Patricia (trans.), 'Völuspá', *The Poetic Edda (Poems of the Vikings: The Elder Edda)*, (1990: University of Pennsylvania Press).

Tønnessen, Johan N. and Arne Odd Johnsen, *The History of Modern Whaling*, trans. R.I. Christophersen (Berkeley, 1982: University of California Press).

APPENDIX

WHALING OFF THE COAST OF IRELAND.

BY CRAWFORD HARTNELL.

WE left the Broadstone Terminus of the Midland Great Western Railway at seven o'clock one fine morning last autumn, *en route* for Innishkea South—an island some fourteen miles from Achill, Dugort. The railway had brought us to Achill Sound, the long car to Dugort and a little cutter took us on to Innishkea, where we arrived before nightfall. Three old sailing men formed the party, and the reason of their journey West was supplied by the prospect of a whaling expedition in Irish waters. Some enterprising Norwegians had established the fishery, and erected one factory in Innishkea, and there was already a rumour that the success of the undertaking justified the building of a second. Between the two islands—Innishkea North and Innishkea South—was a much smaller island, and here—amazing sight—amidst such surroundings, we found many buildings, hives of industry, one, with a tall factory chimney, with its crown of smoke. These buildings, the headquarters of the first whaling station opened in Ireland for over a century and a quarter, included, amongst others, a whale oil refinery, where the blubber, when "flenched" off the carcase, was rendered into a chocolate coloured oil by boiling; a meat house for treating whale flesh, and a mill where the meat was kiln dried, and converted into decorticated cattle food, two kilos of which daily perform wonders in Norway, fattening stock, and increasing the yield of milk from dairy cattle. There was also a bonehouse, where the huge frame structure of the whale was dried, and made into bonemeal for use as a fertilizer. A few frame houses were devoted to the needs of the staff.

The Island of Innishkea South, with a whale floating in the foreground. From a snapshot by E. T. Pasley, L.D.S.I.

At the anchorage lay three steamers of varying tonnage, and beyond them, what looked like a much smaller island, but proved to be a number of dead whales moored ready for the attention of the operatives at the factory. The morning was dark and chill as we passed to the beach, two islanders carrying our coracle upon their heads, like an exaggeration of a fashionable hat, and launching her, with a loud splash, through the surf. We were just in time, for our steamer was on the point of departure; indeed, the anchor chains were already singing through the hawse pipes, and as soon as we had clambered up the side of the vessel, crossed the rail, and got our belongings on board, she was churning her way down the sound towards the ocean.

Steamer working on the Innishkea Station, with a number of dead whales. From a snapshot by E. T. Pasley, L.D.S.I.

The whaling steamer, built specially for this work, was a compact, comfortable, capital sailor's ship, ninety-six feet in length. Right aft was the tiny saloon, bright in white enamel and gilt, with two fine staterooms—one of them the captain's quarters. Forward of the saloon the engines were installed, and these gave the trim little Norwegian-built vessel a speed of about 11 knots per hour. Immediately in front of the engines—but on the deck level—stood the cook's galley and the mess-house, where the Captain and any guest of his ate their meals—mostly appetising Norwegian dishes—sweet fruit soup, fried sayce, "lobscouse," and other capital delicacies for hungry men, especially when washed down with the best coffee in the world, as it seemed to us that raw, chill morning. Overhead was the chart-room, a cosy apartment, and in front the wheel, speaking tube to engines, a telegraph with all the wordings in Norwegian, and the bridge. Immediately forward of the bridge, but on the deck level, stood a powerful winch, having two big drums at either side, the forward drums being indented with five broad channels to receive the cable, the after drums with six. A cable of finest Italian hemp, six inches in circumference, and so elastic that, under heavy strain, it stretched to almost half its normal bulk, was delivered from a conical structure on the deck. This cable, which was coiled in the hold, was fed through the conical structure, to the winch, where it passed over and under the two grooved drums on the port side, and then forward to the bow.

In the bow was fixed a raised platform, which extended about eight feet aft. The centre of this platform was occupied by a formidable cannon, measuring some four feet six inches in length, and pierced by a 3½-inch bore. The cannon was mounted on a broad circular iron column fixed in the deck, and was flanked at either side by a hinged plank in the flooring of the platform. Through the channel beneath the lid so formed the cable passed to the bow, and was laid over a revolving brass sheave, the end of the cable being coiled several times upon a flat round iron shield, which was placed at an inclined angle beneath the muzzle of the gun. The end of the cable was spliced to the shaft of the harpoon, the foremost portion of which projected from the gun, and the gun, working on a pivot, could be depressed or elevated to any angle, and slewed to port or starboard with equal ease and facility.

The gun, which had a high sight running from end to end, was charged with a bag of pebble powder, weighing possibly two pounds, and wadded with a few handfuls of hempen waste, the entire charge being tamped home with a thin circular layer of cork, cut exactly to the size of the bore. The harpoon was now placed in the gun. It was made of wrought-iron, and weighed seven stone five pounds. The base of the harpoon fitted the bore loosely, and about a third of the projectile's entire length protruded from the muzzle. The protruding portion of the projectile was armed with four formidable barbs, loose at the end nearest to the muzzle, and hinged forward, with a powerful spring hinge, to the shaft of the harpoon nearer the point. The loose ends were firmly lashed down. Above the hinges was a stout, hollow, iron tube, with a broad screw thread on the outer side. In this hollow tube a copper clad fuse was deposited. A hollow iron conical head, ending in a solid iron spear-like termination, was filled with coarse blasting powder, and this head, or cap, as it is called, was screwed over the tube containing the fuse. Behind the barbs the cable was spliced on. The range of the gun is uncertain, but a shot is rarely fired at a greater distance than 50 yards.

About 10 a.m., when some 60 miles out, the vessel then being on the edge of the Atlantic deep water, the look-out man in the barrel-shaped crow's nest, fixed securely to the starboard side of the mast, boomed out the word "Goon," and indicated the direction by a gesture. "Goon" was called through the brass tube, the engines responded instantly, and the vessel ploughed through the Atlantic at her best. The sun was now up, and the smooth water danced under its rays like a sea of molten silver. The captain was instantly upon the roof of the chart room with his glass, a hurried observation, a word to the mate, who was at the wheel, and the next minute our skipper was alongside the man in the crow's nest, appearing a few moments later upon the gun platform at the bow.

The fish was now in full sight. He was travelling at a right angle to the vessel's course. On he came, blowing a cloud of vapour into the air. His approach appeared almost leisurely—first emerged the huge head, with its enormous mouth, up and upward, until half his length appeared, showing the long five-foot side fins, slate blue upon the upper sides, glittering white beneath, and then the head was directed downwards, and the remainder of the body was revealed, terminating in the great fluked tail. Three leisurely dives of this character terminated in the fish going down "sounding" for a short interval.

"Sagte," pronounced "Sacta," and meaning Slow, had been called by the captain from the gun platform, and instantly repeated from the bridge to the engine room, at the second dive, and as the fish went down again the order was given, this time dead slow, and the vessel crept at a snail's pace towards the spot where experience anticipated the re-appearance of the monster. It seemed an age, but was, in fact, only a few brief minutes, ere the huge head and the forepart of the body was again revealed. The fish turned slowly. At length a satisfactory position was attained, and the gun boomed out. A miss! The swirl of the great tail struck the harpoon, and turned it aside, and the leviathan passed on in safety.

The gun was rapidly re-charged, and almost immediately the second fish was sighted. The lithe, athletic form of our young captain, a debonnair, bright specimen of fine young manhood, whose fair hair and moustache and brilliant blue eyes told his nationality, stood beside his gun, and as our second fish came up, after his five minutes interval, the trigger was pulled—"Boom!" and the harpoon was launched with its following tail of cable, running out in a zig-zag, like a streak of hempen lightning.

Our luck, for the moment, was both out and in that morning. Out, for the harpoon, although it struck the fish, did so unequally, and when it was brought aboard one of the barbs was twisted. In, because the fish missed us as we had missed him, for, as he dived, he delivered a tremendous blow of his tail at the vessel's bow, and happily struck short.

This closed the ill-luck for the day. Another whale was shortly sighted, and our third shot struck the creature between the fin and the eye, piercing the side. Three seconds after the impact the conical cap, or bomb, exploded in the fish, tearing open a mighty wound in the side, and at the same moment bursting the lashings and releasing the four barbs which, springing forward in the flesh, prevent the harpoon being disengaged or withdrawn. Indeed the harpoon remains in the fish until cut out at the factory. The fish was killed outright by the explosion and sank, our cable tearing out over the winch, which was enveloped in smoke, caused by the friction of an immense block of hard oak. This block, working in the grooved wheel of the winch, acted as a powerful brake upon its progress. After an interval the winch was reversed, and steadily the cable came inboard, ultimately bringing the whale to the bow. A double-weighted line was now thrown beneath the flukes of the great tail, which was hauled up to the bow; a heavy fluke chain was bolted on beneath the tail, which was elevated above the rail. A sharp, hoe-like instrument, with a long handle, was next employed to cut away the flukes of the tail, which is composed of solid gristle, enough being left to insure that the chain would not slip over the remnant and release the dead fish. The huge body floated alongside the steamer's hull, the head lying against her side, although secured only by the chain at the tail. A lance was now brought. This lance had a sharp, solid head attached to a hollow shaft, which, for about eighteen inches of its length, was pierced with holes like a colander. To the upper end of the hollow shaft a rubber tube was attached, and this tube was led aft to the engine room. The belly of the whale was next pierced with the lance, which was imbedded in the flesh and pressed home until all the perforations had disappeared in the body. This being accomplished, the engines at once pumped the fish full of air, so that the great body, thus given additional buoyancy, floated half above the water level. The lance was now withdrawn, and its perforation caulked with a wad of tow, so that the escape of air was prevented.

"Goon," boomed from the crow's nest, just as this operation had been completed. In a minute of time a large white barrel buoy was got upon deck. To this buoy, which bore the vessel's "fishing number," a long bamboo mast had been affixed, and from the mast three brightly-coloured flags of the International Code fluttered gaily. The barrel and mast were now made fast to the whale, which was cast adrift, and off we went in hot pursuit of the leviathan that had just been sighted.

This, the last "shot" of the day, was also secured. Struck, however, between the tail and the fin in a less vital part, he at once dashed forward through the water. The vessel was steaming at about eleven knots but the whale raced ahead, breaking the water into miniature "seas" and spouting aloft torrents of blood and vapour. On and onward we dashed until the vessel, although under a full head of steam, no longer relied upon her engines for her momentum, but travelled ahead at tremendous pace, towed by her maddened capture. But the race was not to be to the swift, and when about a thousand fathoms of line had been run out to sea, the speed slackened, and once more the engines were creating the pace. The fish growing weaker and weaker, at length ceased his herculean exertions, the winch was reversed and the capture was steadily drawn towards the vessel. An ingenious device now helped the process of final exhaustion as the fish came in.

Immediately following the death struggle, or "flurry" of the whales a shoal of dolphins appeared, sporting and gambolling round the vessel, and an unsuccessful effort was made to bag one with a rifle as the fish sprang gracefully from the water into the air.

The vessel headed back, picked up the first whale which had been buoyed and cast adrift. This was secured upon the starboard side, and thus weighted, the vessel, now travelling little over five knots an hour, steamed for the moorings at Innishkea. Within 36 hours of leaving Broadstone, Dublin, we had assisted at the killing of the two whales, and with our booty in tow we were homeward bound. Just before six o'clock next morning the steamer entered the Sound and cast anchor alongside a mammoth larder, where the catch of the day was moored. Here the leviathiane lay awaiting dismantlement. The larger of our two catches was towed to the great broad white wooden stage at the factory, and there drawn up by winches to be "stripped" at once, for the fresh blubber makes the better oil. Here we inspected him closely as he lay upon his back on the stage, picking our steps with great caution, for the stage with its surfacing of oil and grease, was more slippery than ice, and we were obliged to walk with great circumspection least the corrugations of our rubber sea boots would be inadequate to secure foothold on the treacherous surface over which the accustomed workers skated, with grace, in safety. The fish was now measured with huge wooden callipers. In length the body was four inches short of 65 feet. The skilled manager of the factory estimated that the weight of the fish would be about 25 tons. The tongue, we were told, would probably scale tons, but the eye, so disproportioned was the creature, barely measured three inches from corner to corner, and was just two, or two and a half inches across. With the fish lying upon its back a six-foot man could just touch the lower eyelid.

Around the huge mouth was ranged the baleen or whalebone, which hung from the lip in triangular-shaped sheets, with a long fringe of whalebone hair, used as a strainer, at the lower edge. This fringed whalebone filled the entire space between the jaws, the sheets being set vertically and on edge along the upper lip, like louvre boards in the ventilating window of a church steeple. The fish was a Balenoptera Sibbaldii or "Blue Whale," so called from its colour—slate blue, dabbled with irregular patches of white and white pink. From its under lip to the belly the fish was covered with large raised corrugations, like nothing so much as great railway tracks of india-rubber, and these, to continue the simile, were connected at intervals with joinings, resembling the points upon the track of a railroad. The remainder of the body was quite smooth. The blubber was cut, or "flenched" away in lengths and thick strips by the aid of a winch, and rendered into whale oil, that most perfect of lubricants, which was then barrelled for shipment. The flesh was, if somewhat richer, not much inferior to the coarser kinds of foreign beef, which it closely resembled. It is used as a food in parts of Germany and Russia. This Norwegian-Irish factory, however, being far from these markets, converts the flesh into cattle food, and the bones and offal into guano. The whalebone of the blue whale is thin, and of an inferior quality, and only realises some £35 a ton, while the fine whalebone of the Nordkapper (Baloena Biscayensis), one of the two species of "Right" whale, which has also been caught off the Irish coast, fetches the fancy price of ever £1,000 per ton, and a single large fish has been known to yield a quarter of a ton.

Loading the harpoon gun. From a snap shot by E. T. Pasley, L.D.S.I.

The most valuable whale oil—spermaceti—is contained in an oblong cistern in the head of the cachalot or sperm whale (Physote Macrocephalos). The oil next in value is derived from the blubber of the sperm whale. This variety, several of which have been taken at this fishery during the present season, is without whalebone, but is furnished with a set of teeth, each shapel like a cucumber, and as white as ivory. These teeth are in the lower jaw only, the upper jaw being provided with cavities to receive the teeth. The teeth realise about ten shillings apiece, and the total value of a large sperm whale would probably be £300.

Cutting up the blubber at the Innishkea Factory. From a snapshot by E. T. Pasley, L.D.S.I.

The Finner whale (Baloenoptera Musculus) is another variety taken in Irish waters, and is furnished with a whalebone of less value than that yielded by the blue whale. The value of a 68 foot Finner would be about £65.

The vast yard above the wide slip and wooden pier was crowded with whale *debris*, fat, meat and bone, in every stage of demolition, some of the bodies being stripped of their blubber by an army of workers, some having the meat cut away, while others, reduced to mere bone, were being chopped into convenient pieces for the kilns. The stories of the odours arising from the different processes have been much exaggerated, and we suffered no inconvenience whatever, although we minutely inspected the process at every stage.

Our second fish was some half dozen feet shorter than the first, and these delivered, the steamer once more put out to sea. The captain had 39 whales to the credit of his vessel this season, and was eager to complete his forty fish before the threatened break in the weather arrived. His vessel was worked by a Norwegian crew of ten men, fine fellows all, with the coolness of practised seamen, the keenness and special knowledge inherited from long generations of whaling ancestors, and the elan and eagerness of sportsmen. Of the natives of these far Western Irish isles—sons of nature, like themselves—they spoke with an obviously warm regard. They found them "a nice people," a "good people," "a brave people." A similarity of ideas, a simple, cleanly view of life, both representatives of a hardy, brave, courteous, kindly, hospitable race, and each holding deeply religious views—however the dogmas differed—gave them so much in common that the Irishmen and the Norwegians met on level ground, and were leal, fast friends and allies. The blessing the fishery has been to these poor islands cannot be overestimated. The whalers found in them a fine factory site, close to the fishing grounds, where the whale is, given good weather, fairly plentiful from May to September. Safe anchorage, good water, brought in iron pipes from the uplands, a supply of intelligent, industrious labour, and a position not too remote for obtaining supplies of food and fuel, and fairly convenient to the markets for whale products. "Is it true," I asked an intelligent Islander, "that the whaling interferes with the fishing?" "No," he replied, "but the factory pays better than the fishing. The seas are full of fish, but the markets are so far off and the prices so poor! God bless the Norwegians; they have come, and may they stay long." The Islanders all speak Gaelic and English, and are already picking up a few words and phrases from their Norwegian friends and benefactors.

The whaling industry has been an ancient one in Ireland, and the Irish Parliament, which had a close and careful eye for the development of the few trades not hampered by penal restrictions, fostered it intelligently. The first published debates of the Irish Parliament, covering the years 1763-1764, show the efforts made by the Irish Legislature. These debates are the first efforts at Parliamentary reporting, and were the work of one Sir James Caldwell, Bart., and Count of Milan, an English officer stationed in Dublin, who records that he was so fascinated by the eloquence and sound sense of the Irish House of Commons that he attended night after night throughout the sittings, and on his return to quarters after each debate he faithfully recorded the business done, with shrewd comments upon the work performed. In the second volume of these well-known *"Debates (in the Irish House of Commons) Relating to the Affairs of Ireland in the years 1763 and 1764, by a Military Officer"—to which the historians Lecky, Whiteside, and Froude were so much indebted—it is related that the Committee of the whole Irish House granted £1,500 to Nesbit and Company, Killybegs, Co. Donegal, for encouraging whale fishing on the North-Western coast of Ireland, and manufacturing the bone and blubber. One, Chaplain, too, received similar help. He had been a subaltern in the Army stationed at Gibraltar, and had there learned from one of the Nesbit family, who held a captain's commission, that a profitable whaling business might be done in the Irish seas between Sligo Bay and Tyland Head, Donegal. Chaplain, who had experience of the Greenland whale fishery, at once sold his comission, came to Ireland, and the old Irish Parliament granted him £500 to purchase the necessary gear and inaugurate his industry. The Nesbits and the Chaplains, however, found that the system of fishing adopted in the calm waters of Greenland were unsuitable in the heavy seas off Western Ireland, where the water is generally rough. It was found that the hand-thrown harpoon when it struck the fish rarely entered, and in order to give additional force to the harpoon or lance, Nesbit invented a swivel gun from which he contrived to discharge the harpoon. This, the first swivel gun used in whaling, invented for use in the Irish seas, manufactured in Dublin with the money voted by the Irish Parliament, was employed 143 years ago, and with almost instant success. It is strikingly remarkable that the Norwegians have revived in Irish waters the whaling enterprise fostered by the old Irish Parliament, and pursue the work somewhat on the lines adopted by Nesbit and Co. in 1763. It is still more remarkable that some local bodies in the West of Ireland have made the revived industry the object of a foolish hostility.

*Published in London, 1766, Vol II., pp. 413-416.

'Whaling off the coast of Ireland'

Reproduced here with kind permission from *The Irish Times*

WEEKLY IRISH TIMES, SATURDAY, JANUARY 8, 1910

WHALING OFF THE COAST OF IRELAND

BY CRAWFORD HARTNELL

WE left the Broadstone Terminus of the Midland Great Western Railway at seven o' clock one fine morning last autumn, en route for Innishkea South—an island some fourteen miles from Achill, Dugort. The railway had brought us to Achill Sound; the long car to Dugort and a little cutter took us on to Innishkea, where we arrived before nightfall. Three old sailing men formed the party, and the reason of their journey West was supplied by the prospect of a whaling expedition in Irish waters. Some enterprising Norwegians had established the fishery, and erected one factory in Innishkea, and there was already a rumour that the success of the undertaking justified the building of a second. Between the two islands—Innishkea North and Innishkea South—was a much smaller island, and here—amazing sight—amidst such surroundings, we found many buildings, hives of industry, one, with a tall factory chimney, with its crown of smoke. These buildings, the headquarters of the first whaling station opened in Ireland for over a century and a quarter, included, amongst others, a whale oil refinery, where the blubber, when "flenched" off the carcase, was rendered into a chocolate coloured, oil by boiling; a meat house for treating whale flesh, and a mill where the meat was kiln dried, and converted into decorticated cattle food, two kilos of which daily perform wonders in Norway, fattening stock, and increasing the yield of milk from dairy cattle. There was also a bonehouse, where the huge frame structure of the whale was dried, and made into bonemeal for use as a fertilizer. A few frame houses were devoted to the needs of the staff.

At the anchorage lay three steamers of varying tonnage, and beyond them, what looked like a much smaller island, but proved to be a number of dead whales moored ready for the attention of the operatives at the factory. The morning was dark and chill as we passed to the beach, two islanders carrying our coracle upon their heads, like an exaggeration of a fashionable hat, and launching her, with a loud splash, through the surf. We were just in time, for our steamer was on the point of departure; indeed, the anchor chains were already singing through the hawse pipes, and as soon as we had clambered up the side of the vessel, crossed the rail, and got our belongings on board, she was churning her way down the sound towards the ocean. The whaling steamer, built specially for this work, was a compact, comfortable, capital sailor's ship, ninety-six feet in length. Right aft was the tiny saloon, bright in white enamel and gilt, with two fine state-rooms—one of them the captain's quarters. Forward of the saloon the engines were installed, and these gave the trim little Norwegian-built vessel a speed of about 11 knots per hour. Immediately in front of the engines—but on the deck level—stood the cook's galley and the mess-house , where the Captain and any guest of his ate their meals —mostly appetising Norwegian dishes—sweet fruit soup, fried sayce, "lobscuse," and other capital delicacies for hungry men, especially when washed down with the best coffee in the world, as it seemed to us that raw, chill morning. Overhead was the chart-room, a cosy apartment, and in front of the wheel, speaking tube to engines, a telegraph with all the wordings in Norwegian, and the bridge. Immediately forward of the bridge, but on the deck level, stood a powerful winch, having two big drums at either side, the forward drums being indented with five broad channels to receive the cable, the after drums with six. A cable of finest Italian hemp, six inches in circumference, and so elastic that, under heavy strain, it stretched to almost half its normal bulk, was delivered from a conical structure on the deck. This cable, which was coiled in the hold, was fed through the conical structure, to the winch, where it passed over and under the two grooved drums on the port side, and then forward to the bow.

In the bow was fixed a raised platform, which extended about eight feet aft. The centre of this platform was occupied by a formidable cannon, measuring some four feet six inches in length, and pierced by a 31/2 inch bore. The cannon was mounted on a broad circular iron column fixed in the deck, and was flanked at either side by a hinged plank in the flooring of the platform. Through the channel beneath the lid so formed the cable passed to the bow, and was laid over a revolving brass sheave, the end of the cable being coiled several times upon a flat round iron shield, which was placed at an inclined angle beneath the muzzle of the gun. The end of the cable was spliced to the shaft of the harpoon, the foremost portion of which projected from the gun, and the gun, working on a pivot, could be depressed or elevated to any angle, and slewed to port or starboard with equal ease and facility.

The gun. which had a high sight running from end to end, was charged with a bag of pebble powder, weighing possibly two pounds, and wadded with a few handfuls of hempen waste, the entire charge being tamped home with a thin circular layer of cork, cut exactly to the size of the bore. The harpoon was now placed in the gun. It was made of wrought-iron, and weighed seven stone five pounds. The base of the harpoon fitted the bore loosely, and about a third of the projectile's entire length protruded from the muzzle. The protruding portion of the projectile was armed with four formidable barbs, loose at the end nearest to the muzzle, and hinged forward, with a powerful spring hinge, to the shaft of the harpoon nearer the point. The loose ends were firmly lashed down. Above the hinges was a stout, hollow, iron tube, with a broad screw thread on the outer side. In this hollow tube a copper-clad fuse was deposited. A hollow iron conical head, ending in a solid iron spear-like termination, was filled with coarse blasting powder, and this head, or cap, as it is called, was screwed over the tube containing the fuse. Behind the barbs the cable was spliced on. The range of the gun is uncertain; but a shot is rarely fired at a greater distance than 50 yards.

About 10 a.m., when some 60 miles out, the vessel then being on the edge of the Atlantic deep water, the look-out man in the barrel-shaped crow's nest, fixed securely to the starboard side of the mast, boomed out the word "Goon," and indicated the direction by a gesture. "Goon" was called through the brass tube, the engines responded instantly, and the vessel ploughed through the Atlantic at her best. The sun was now up, and the smooth water danced under its rays like a sea of molten silver. The captain was instantly upon the roof of the chart room with his glass, a hurried observation, a word to the mate, who was at the wheel, and the next minute our skipper was alongside the man in the crow's nest, appearing a few moments later upon the gun platform at the bow.

The fish was now in full sight. He was travelling at a right angle to the vessel's course. On he came, blowing a cloud of vapour into the air. His approach appeared almost leisurely—first emerged the huge head, with its enormous mouth, up and upward, until half his length appeared, showing the long five-foot side fins, slate blue upon the upper sides, glittering white beneath, and then the head was directed downwards, and the remainder of the body was revealed, terminating in the great fluked tail. Three leisurely dives of this character terminated in the fish going down "sounding" for a short interval.

"Sagte", pronounced "Sacta," and meaning Slow, had been called by the captain from the gun platform, and instantly repeated from the bridge to the engine room, at the second dive, and as the fish went down again the order was given, this time dead slow, and the vessel crept at a snail's pace towards the spot where experience anticipated the reappearance of the monster. It seemed an age, but was, in fact, only a few brief minutes, ere the huge head and the forepart of the body was again revealed. The fish turned slowly. At length a satisfactory position was attained, and the gun boomed out. A miss! The swirl of the great tail struck the harpoon, and turned it aside, and the leviathan passed on in safety.

The gun was rapidly re-charged, and almost immediately the second fish was sighted! The lithe, athletic form of our young captain, a debonair, bright specimen of fine young manhood, whose fair hair and moustache and brilliant blue eyes told his nationality, stood beside his gun, and as our second fish came up, after his five minutes interval, the trigger was pulled— "Boom!" and the harpoon was launched with its following tail of cable, running out in a zig-zag, like a streak of hempen lightning.

Our luck, for the moment, was both out and |in that morning. Out, for the harpoon, although it struck the fish, did so unequally, and when it was brought aboard one of the barbs was twisted. In, because the fish missed us as we had missed him, for, as he dived, he delivered a tremendous blow of his tail at the vessel's bow, and happily struck short.

This closed the ill-luck for the day. Another whale was shortly sighted, and our third shot struck the creature between the fin and the eye, piercing the side. Three seconds after the impact the conical cap, or bomb, exploded in the fish, tearing open a mighty wound in the side, and at the same moment bursting the lashings and releasing the four barbs which, springing forward in the flesh, prevent the harpoon being disengaged or withdrawn. Indeed the harpoon remains in the fish until cut out at the factory. The fish was killed outright by the explosion and sank, our cable tearing out over the winch, which was enveloped in smoke, caused by the friction of an immense block of hard oak. This block, working in the grooved wheel of the winch, acted as a powerful brake upon its progress. After an interval the winch was reversed, and steadily the cable came inboard, ultimately bringing the whale to the bow. A double-weighted line was now thrown beneath the flukes of the great tail, which was hauled up to the bow; a heavy fluke chain was bolted on beneath the tail, which was elevated above the rail. A sharp, hoe-like instrument, with a long handle, was next employed to cut away the flukes of the tail, which is composed of solid gristle, enough being left to insure that the chain would not slip over the remnant and release the dead fish. The huge body floated alongside the steamer's hull, the head lying against her side, although secured only by the chain at the tail. A lance was now brought. This lance had a sharp, solid head attached to a hollow shaft, which, for about eighteen inches of its length, was pierced with holes like a colander. To the upper end of the hollow shaft a rubber tube was attached, and this tube was led aft to the engine room. The belly of the whale was next pierced with the lance, which was embedded in the fish and pressed home until all the perforations had disappeared in the body. This being accomplished, the engines at once pumped the fish full of air, so that the great body, thus given additional buoyancy, floated half above the water level. The lance was now withdrawn, and its perforation caulked with a wad of tow, so that the escape of air was prevented.

"Goon," boomed from the crow's nest, just as this operation had been completed. In a minute of time a large white barrel buoy was got upon deck. To this buoy, which bore the vessel's "fishing number," a long bamboo mast had been affixed, and from the mast three brightly-coloured flags of the International Code fluttered gaily. The barrel and mast were now made fast to the whale, which was cast adrift, and off we went in hot pursuit of the leviathan that had just been sighted.

This, the last "shot" of the day, was also secured. Struck, however, between the tail and the fin in a less vital part, he at once dashed forward through the water. The vessel was steaming at about eleven knots but the whale raced ahead, breaking the water into miniature "seas" and spouting aloft torrents of blood and vapour. On and onward we dashed until the vessel, although under a full head of steam, no longer relied upon her engines for her momentum, but travelled ahead at tremendous pace, towed by her maddened capture. But the race was not to be to the swift , and when about a thousand fathoms of line had been run out to sea, the speed slackened, and once more the engines were creating the pace. The fish growing weaker and weaker, at length ceased his herculean exertions, the winch was reversed and the capture was steadily drawn towards the vessel. An ingenious device now helped the process of final exhaustion as the fish came in.

Immediately following the death struggle, or "flurry" of the whales a shoal of dolphins appeared, sporting and gambolling round the vessel, and an unsuccessful effort was made to bag one with a rifle as the fish sprang gracefully from the water into the air.

The vessel headed back, picked up the first whale which had been buoyed and cast adrift. This was secured upon the starboard side, and thus weighted, the vessel, now travelling little over five knots an hour, steamed for the moorings at Innishkea. Within 36 hours of leaving Broadstone, Dublin, we had assisted at the killing of the two whales, and with our booty in tow we were homeward bound. Just before six o' clock next morning the steamer entered the Sound and cast anchor alongside a mammoth larder, where the catch of the day was moored. Here the leviathans lay awaiting dismantlement. The larger of our two catches was towed to the great broad white wooden stage at the factory, and there drawn up by winches to be "stripped" at once, for the fresh blubber makes the better oil. Here we inspected him closely as he lay upon his back on the stage, picking our steps with great caution, for the stage with its surfacing of oil and grease, was more slippery than ice, and we were obliged to walk with great circumspection least the corrugations of our rubber sea boots would be inadequate to secure foothold on the treacherous surface, over which the accustomed workers skated, with grace, in safety. The fish was now measured with huge wooden callipers. In length the body was four inches short of 65 feet. The skilled manager of the factory estimated that the weight of the fish would be about 25 tons. The tongue, we were told, would probably scale tons, but the eye, so disproportionate was the creature, barely measured three inches from corner to corner, and was just two, or two and a half inches across. With the fish lying upon its back a six-foot man could touch the lower eyelid.

Around the huge mouth was ranged the baleen or whalebone, which hung from the lip in triangular-shaped sheets, with a long fringe of whalebone hair, used as a strainer, at the lower edge. This fringed whalebone filled the entire space between the jaws, the sheets being set vertically and on edge along the upper lip, like louvre boards in the ventilating window of a church steeple. The fish was a Balenoptera Sibbaldii or "Blue Whale," so called from its colour—slate blue, dabbled with irregular patches of white and white pink. From its under lip to the belly the fish was covered with large raised corrugations, like nothing so much as great railway tracks of india-rubber, and these, to continue the simile, were connected at intervals with joinings, resembling the points upon the track of a railroad. The remainder of the body was quite smooth. The blubber was cut, or "flenched" away in lengths and thick strips by the aid of a winch, and rendered into whale oil, that most perfect of lubricants, which was then barrelled for shipment. The flesh was, if somewhat richer, not much inferior to the coarser kinds of foreign beef, which it closely resembled. It is used as a food in parts of Germany and Russia. This Norwegian-Irish factory, however, being far from these markets, converts the flesh into cattle food, and the bones and offal into guano. The whalebone of the blue whale is thin, and of an inferior quality, and only realises some £35 a ton, while the fine whalebone of the Nordkapper (Baloena Biscayensis), one of the two species of "Right" whale, which has also been caught off the Irish coast, fetches the fancy price of ever £1,000 per ton, and a single large fish has been known to yield a quarter of a ton.

The most valuable whale oil—spermaceti— is contained in an oblong cistern m the head of the cachalot or sperm whale (Physote Macrocephalos). The oil next in value was derived from the blubber of the sperm whale. This variety, several of which have been taken at this fishery during the present season, is without whalebone, but is furnished with a set of teeth, each shapel like a cucumber, and as white as ivory. These teeth are in the lower jaw only, the upper jaw being provided with cavities to receive the teeth. The teeth realise about ten shillings apiece, and the total value of a large sperm whale would probably be £300.

The Finner whale (Baloenoptera Musculus) is another variety taken in Irish waters, and is furnished with a whalebone of less value than that yielded by the blue whale. The value of a 68 foot Finner would be about £65.

The vast yard above the wide slip and wooden pier was crowded with whale debris, fat, meat and bone, in every stage of demolition, some of the bodies being stripped of their blubber by an army of workers, some having the meat cut away, while others, reduced to mere bone, were being chopped into convenient pieces for the kilns. The stories of the odours arising from the different processes have been much exaggerated, and we suffered no inconvenience whatever, although we minutely inspected the process at every stage.

Our second fish was some half dozen feet shorter than the first, and these delivered, the steamer once more put out to sea. The captain had 39 whales to the credit of his vessel this season, and was eager to complete his forty fish before the threatened break in the weather arrived. His vessel was worked by a Norwegian crew of ten men, fine fellows all, with the coolness of practised seamen, the keenness and special knowledge inherited from long generations of whaling ancestors, and the- elan and eagerness of sportsmen. Of the natives of these far Western Irish isles—sons of nature, like themselves—they spoke with an obviously warm regard. They found them "a nice people," a "good people," a "brave people." A similarity of ideas, a simple cleanly view of life, both representatives of a hardy, brave, courteous, kindly, hospitable race, and each holding deeply religious views—however the dogmas differed—gave them so much in common that the Irishmen and Norwegians met on level ground, and were leal, fast friends and allies. The blessing the fishery has been to these poor islands cannot be overestimated. The whalers found in them a fine factory site, close to the fishing grounds, where the whale is, given good weather, fairly plentiful from May to September. Safe anchorage, good water, brought in iron pipes from the uplands, a supply of intelligent, industrious labour, and a position not too remote for obtaining supplies of food and fuel, and fairly convenient to the markets for whale products. "Is it true, " I asked an intelligent Islander, "that the whaling interferes with the fishing?" "No," he " replied, "but the factory pays better than tin fishing. The seas are full of fish, but the markets are so far off and the prices so poor! God bless the Norwegians; they have come, and may they stay long." The Islanders speak Gaelic and English, and are already picking up a few words and phrases from their Norwegian friends and benefactors.

The whaling industry has been an ancient one in Ireland, and the Irish Parliament which had a close and careful eye for the development of a few trades not hampered by penal restrictions, fostered it intelligently. The first published debates of the Irish Parliament, covering the years 1763-1764, show the efforts made by the Irish Legislature. These debates are the first efforts at Parliamentary reporting, and were the work of one Sir James Caldwell, Bart., and Count of Milan, an English officer stationed in Dublin, who records that he was so fascinated by the eloquence and sound sense of the Irish House of Commons that he attended night after night throughout the sittings, and on his return to quarters after each debate he faithfully recorded the business done, with shrewd comments upon the work performed. In the second volume of these well-known "'Debates in the Irish House of Commons Relating to the Affairs of Ireland in the years 1763 and 1764, by a Military Officer'"* - to which the historians Lecky, Whiteside, and Froude were so much indebted—it is related that the Committee of the whole Irish House granted £1,500 to Nesbit and Company, Killybegs, Co. Donegal, for encouraging whale fishing on the North-Western coast of Irelandand manufacturing the bow and blubber. One, Chaplain too, received similar help. He had been a subaltern in the Army stationed at Gibraltar, and had there learned from one of the Nesbit family, who held a captain's commission, that a profitable whaling business might be done in the Irish seas between Sligo Bay and Tyland Head, Donegal. Chaplain, who had experience of the Greenland whale fishery, at once sold his commission, came to Ireland, and the old Irish Parliament granted him £500 to purchase the necessary gear and inaugurate his industry. The Nesbits and the Chaplains, however, found that the system of fishing adopted in the calm waters of Greenly were unsuitable in the heavy seas off Western Ireland, where the water is generally rough. It was found that the hand-thrown harpoon, when it struck the fish rarely entered, and in order to give additional force to the harpoon or lance, Nesbit invented a swivel gun from which he contrived to discharge the harpoon. This, the first swivel gun used in whaling, invented for use in the Irish seas, manufactured in Dublin with the moneys voted by the Irish Parliament, was employed 143 years ago, and with almost instant success. It is striking remarkable that the Norwegians have revived in Irish waters the whaling enterprise fostered by the old Irish Parliament, and pursue the work somewhat on the lines adopted by Nesbit and Co. in 1763. It is still more remarkable that some local bodies in the West of Ireland have made the revived industry the object of a foolish hostility.

---

*Published in London, 1766, Vol II, pp 413-416 3416.

NOTES

1. This book would not be possible without the thorough research of Dr James Fairley, not only in his book *Irish Whales and Whaling*, but also the interview transcripts which he left on public record.

2. Images from Gary Burrows, Marcus Hogan, Brendan Quinn, and Angela Kelly were donated for use in the book to illustrate the whales in their natural habitat. These images were taken on research trips.

3. The whale on page 67 has been identified by Conor Ryan as a blue whale.

4. The poems 'Butchering Shanty' and 'Sons of the Silent Shore' were written to the melody of songs by the the Bard of Erris, Riocard Bairéad (1740–1819).

5. The section headings 'Of Iron and Timber' and 'Of Storm and Water' refer to a piece of folklore from the area provided by Turas Siar called The Seafarer's Warning. It is reproduced here:

> Around the year 1900, Henry Kane from Cartron, a well-known sea trader and merchant, ran a family shop and store in the village. He had to make the treacherous journey once every few weeks from Cartron Harbour to Westport Quay to pick up a boatload of provisions and sail back home with his twelve-ton sail boat laden down with flour, maize, tea and sugar and any other merchandise they sold in the shop. He had four sons, Pat, Jim, Stephen and Harry. On any of those occasions at least three of his sons would accompany him on the journey and help load the stuff at Westport Quay.
>
> In order to make the journey to Westport faster, he would be relying on going with the tide and the current would assist him – this was also very important in passing through Achill Sound and under the bridge from Blacksod Bay into Clew Bay, and again to get as close as possible to the landings at Westport Quay, and the same applied on the return journey – he would have to be mindful of the flowing tide to get in as close as possible to his own private landing pier at Cartron.
>
> Sometimes this didn't work out according to plan because of the changing wind and depending on how many times the boat would have to tack in order to get into the bay. Often the tide could be on the way out again when the boat landed in Cartron Bay.
>
> He would have to drop anchor and wait for the tide to go out so the boat would lie on the strand, then horses and carts as well as

donkeys and creels, and some men and women, carried bags of flour and meal on their backs for anything up to half a mile. If the boat hadn't been completely unloaded, currachs were used on the return tide to take off the rest of the cargo.

On spring tides, the boat was able to dock alongside his own pier, which was situated close to his own house in a spot known to the villagers as 'the landing'. That pier, which had survived for well over one hundred years, was in regular use up until the year 2000, but is no longer there. It was desecrated by council workers during repairs to the storm wall a few years ago. The orders to do this, were given by a local and on nobody's authority but his own.

Sometimes Henry and his sons sailed out of Cartron Bay as early as two or three o'clock in the morning in order to catch the tide at Achill Sound and Westport.

However, on one such occasion the forecast wasn't good. They set out in the usual way. The wind was south easterly and after several tacks they were on their way into Bull's Mouth when Henry spotted another boat sailing close up beside him.

The captain of the other boat shouted across to Henry, 'What sort of boat have you got?' Henry shouted back to him, 'A boat of iron and timber,' and then Henry asked him the same question, to which he replied, 'A boat of storm and water.'

Immediately Henry knew that this wasn't a real-life boat or captain. Then he angrily shouted back to Henry, 'For God's sake, turn back immediately!'

He obeyed his command and sailed as quickly as ever he could back to Cartron Harbour, and just as they were dropping the anchor, a ferocious storm struck. They hurriedly got into the currach and with a great struggle made the short distance to the shore.

The morning turned out so bad that it ripped the thatch off some of the roofs of the houses in the village. Phantom boats and currachs as well as mysterious lights were often encountered with seafarers along this coast. These sightings were accepted as warning signs against imminent danger.

Glossary

For over a thousand years, the Irish, the Scandinavians, and the whales have been unknowingly connected. When Vikings were hunting whales in Irish waters, and marauding and settling along the Irish coast, Old Norse poetry was being written that would give us kennings such as the whale road. Kennings are compound phrases that use figurative language instead of a single noun. From this same era came the *Immrama*, the Old Irish stories of a hero's journey at sea leading to an enisled Otherworld.

We would like to thank Pap Murphy and Tomás Bán Ó Raghallaigh for their Irish translations and the conversations which informed our understanding of the people we wrote about. Their translations are in the Erris dialect of the Irish language. The phrase *Immram Miolbhádorí* was devised to pay homage to the original immrama using Tomás' in-depth knowledge of island phraseology.

While we are not bilingual, we wanted to give some indication of the role language played at the stations and in how the whalers and islanders interacted. Three languages were being spoken, with minimal overlap.

We have done our utmost to honour the native language of our country and its people. Any mistakes are entirely our own.

Old Norse

hron-rād: whale road

hvala blástr: a whale blow

mél-regn: iron rain

hvalfanger: whaler

hamnavoe: safe haven or home port

Irish

agus an cúr – and the froth on the strand

agus long báite, agus na Lochlannaigh, ar bord a gcuid galtáin…
and drowned/ships and the Vikings aboard their galleys

airneál – wind

an bruth – the surf

an ciúnáil – the calm that follows a storm at sea

an fharraige mór – the big sea

an míol mór – the whale

anois, ar ais arís – now, back again

ar an gcladach – on the shore

ar bord libh – all aboard

bádorí na míolta móra – the whaleboatmen

bristeacha – strong waves breaking

caibleadh – spirit voices heard over the sea

caithfidh an fharraige a cuid fhéin a fháil –
the sea must get its own share

caoirleach – timber

créatúr – creature

crugaí – tholepins

féach anois – look now

immram miolbhádorí – voyage of the whaleboatmen

lán mara – flood tide

muca – pigs

ná beidh a leithéidí arís ann – their like shall never be seen again

rí – king

tráigha – ebb tide

tuaim – a natural sound of the ocean against the land

≋

Acknowledgements

The authors wish to express their utmost thanks to the following people.

David Brennan of Mayo Books Press for your immediate enthusiasm for this unusual project. Edwin McGreal and Siobhán Foody for their dedicated production and design, and endless patience.

We are indebted to the work of Dr James Fairley, Richard Ellis, and Rita Nolan, whose books, alongside primary sources and interviews, informed the historical aspect of this work, and to librarian Austin Vaughan for taking the time to show us where to look in the very early days of research.

The Irish Whale and Dolphin Group, in particular Gemma O'Connor and Simon Berrow. Thank you to Conor Ryan for your generous interview. Much of the information in this book is only available because of the tireless work of scientists and volunteers.

The Johnson Museum, National Museum of Ireland, The Irish Film Institute, the National Library of Ireland, *The Irish Times*, Mayo libraries, and Public Record Office of Northern Ireland.

Photographers Gary Burrows, Brendan Quinn, Angela Kelly, Marcus Hogan, Paul Kinsella, and to Anthony Leonard for the generous provision of his grandfather's images.

Tomás Bán Ó Raghallaigh, and to Pap and Kathryn Murphy of Turas Siar culture and heritage centre, for your enthusiasm and generosity from the first step. Alongside primary and secondary sources, interviews with Tomás and Pap informed much of the writing on the Mayo whaling stations.

Declan Kilgannon and crew of *Kiwi Girl* sport fishing for bringing us to meet the humpbacks. To Michael Keane of Blacksod Sea Safari, and the Lavelles of Inishkea Boat Charters for bringing us to Inishkea.

Mayo Arts Office and Creative Ireland, and to Creative Communities Mayo.

Easkey Britton, Philip Hoare, Manchán Magan, Anja Murray, and Mark Nowak, for their time and generous words.

The many people who gave their time, knowledge, and support while we were working on this book, including: Seanín Hughes, Theo O'Grady, Patrick Dexter, Sarah O'Toole, all at the Linenhall Arts Centre, Solas Tourism Hub, and the Wild Atlantic Words festival.

Our friends and family who have been listening to our obsession for the last several years, and will no doubt have to hear about it for several more.

About the authors

Alice Kinsella is a writer from Mayo.

She is the author of poetry pamphlet *Sexy Fruit* (Broken Sleep, 2018), and *Milk: on motherhood and madness* (Picador, 2023). She co-edited *Empty House: poetry and prose on the climate crisis* (Doire Press, 2021). Her debut full-length poetry collection, *The Ethics of Cats*, will be published in 2025. She is an Arts Council of Ireland Next Generation Artist.

Daniel Wade is a writer from Dublin.

In January 2017, his play The Collector opened the 20th anniversary season of the New Theatre, Dublin. In January 2020, his radio drama Crossing the Red Line was broadcast on RTÉ Radio 1 Extra. He is the author of the poetry collections *Iceberg Relief* (Underground Voices, 2017), *Rapids* (Finishing Line Press, 2021), and the novel *A Land Without Wolves* (Temple Dark Books, 2021).

≈